Deleuze and Guattari's
A Thousand Plateaus

READER'S GUIDES

Bloomsbury *Reader's Guides* are clear, concise and accessible introductions to key texts in literature and philosophy. Each book explores the themes, context, criticism and influence of key works, providing a practical introduction to close reading, guiding students towards a thorough understanding of the text. They provide an essential, up-to-date resource, ideal for undergraduate students.

Reader's Guides available

Aristotle's Metaphysics, Edward Halper
Aristotle's Politics, Judith A. Swanson and C. David Corbin
Badiou's Being and Event, Christopher Norris
Berkeley's Principles of Human Knowledge, Alasdair Richmond
Berkeley's Three Dialogues, Aaron Garrett
Deleuze and Guattari's What is Philosophy?, Rex Butler
Deleuze's Difference and Repetition, Joe Hughes
Derrida's Writing and Difference, Sarah Wood
Hegel's Phenomenology of Spirit, Stephen Houlgate
Heidegger's Later Writings, Lee Braver
Hume's Enquiry Concerning Human Understanding, Alan Bailey and Dan O'Brien
Kant's Critique of Aesthetic Judgement, Fiona Hughes
Kierkegaard's Fear and Trembling, Clare Carlisle
Kuhn's The Structure of Scientific Revolutions, John Preston
Locke's Essay Concerning Human Understanding, William Uzgalis
Machiavelli's The Prince, Miguel Vatter
Mill's Utilitarianism, Henry R. West
Nietzsche's Beyond Good and Evil, Christa Davis Acampora and Keith Ansell Pearson
Nietzsche's The Birth of Tragedy, Douglas Burnham and Martin Jesinghausen
Nietzsche's Thus Spoke Zarathustra, Clancy Martin and Daw-Nay Evans
Plato's Republic, Luke Purshouse
Plato's Symposium, Thomas L. Cooksey
Rawls's A Theory of Justice, Frank Lovett
Sartre's Being and Nothingness, Sebastian Gardner
Schopenhauer's The World as Will and Representation, Robert L. Wicks
Wittgenstein's Philosophical Investigations, Arif Ahmed

A READER'S GUIDE

Deleuze and Guattari's *A Thousand Plateaus*

EUGENE W. HOLLAND

BLOOMSBURY ACADEMIC
LONDON • NEW YORK • OXFORD • NEW DELHI • SYDNEY

BLOOMSBURY ACADEMIC
Bloomsbury Publishing Plc
50 Bedford Square, London, WC1B 3DP, UK
1385 Broadway, New York, NY 10018, USA

BLOOMSBURY, BLOOMSBURY ACADEMIC and the Diana logo are trademarks
of Bloomsbury Publishing Plc

First published 2013
Reprinted by Bloomsbury Academic 2013, 2014, 2016 (twice), 2018, 2019, 2020

Copyright © 2013 Eugene W. Holland

Eugene W. Holland has asserted his right under the Copyright, Designs and Patents
Act, 1988, to be identified as Author of this work.

All rights reserved. No part of this publication may be reproduced or transmitted
in any form or by any means, electronic or mechanical, including photocopying,
recording, or any information storage or retrieval system, without prior permission
in writing from the publishers.

Bloomsbury Publishing Plc does not have any control over, or responsibility for, any
third-party websites referred to or in this book. All internet addresses given in this
book were correct at the time of going to press. The author and publisher regret any
inconvenience caused if addresses have changed or sites have ceased to exist, but
can accept no responsibility for any such changes.

A catalogue record for this book is available from the British Library.

Library of Congress Cataloging-in-Publication Data
Holland, Eugene W.
Deleuze and Guattari's A thousand plateaus: a reader's guide/Eugene W. Holland.
pages cm. – (Reader's guides)
Includes bibliographical references and index.
ISBN 978-0-8264-2302-3 (pbk.: alk. paper) – ISBN 978-0-8264-6576-4 (hardcover: alk.
paper) – ISBN 978-1-4411-6250-2 (ebook (pdf)) – ISBN 978-1-4411-1230-9
(ebook (epub) 1. Deleuze, Giles, 1925-1995. Mille plateaux. 2. Philosophy.
3. Psychoanalysis. 4. Radicalism. 5. Postmodernism. 6. Deleuze, Giles, 1925-1995.
7. Guattari, Felix, 1039-1992. I. Title.
B77.D43H65 2013
194-dc23
2013015956

ISBN: HB: 978-0-8264-6576-4
PB: 978-0-8264-2302-3
ePDF: 978-1-4411-6250-2
eBook: 978-1-4411-1230-9

Series: Reader's Guides

Typeset by Fakenham Prepress Solutions, Fakenham, Norfolk NR21 8NN
Printed and bound in Great Britain

To find out more about our authors and books visit www.bloomsbury.com
and sign up for our newsletters.

CONTENTS

Acknowledgments vii

1 *A Thousand Plateaus* in Context 1
2 Overview of Themes 15
3 Reading the Text 33
4 Reception and Influence 139
5 Further Reading 149

Notes 159
Bibliography 163
Index 175

ACKNOWLEDGMENTS

I would like to thank the following for their helpful feedback on this project in various stages of its development: the students in my seminars at Ohio State (2010) and UC Irvine (2012); the organizers and participants at the Philosophy and Literature Conference at Purdue University (2010), the Fourth International Deleuze Studies conference in Copenhagen, Denmark (2011), and the Kaifeng International Deleuze Conference in Kaifeng, China (2012); Sarah Campbell and her successors at Continuum/Bloomsbury Academic; and, as always, my inimitable "in-house" editor and interlocutor, Eliza Segura-Holland.

Columbus, Ohio
Newport Beach, California

Author note: All page references following quotations in the text refer to *A Thousand Plateaus* unless indicated otherwise.

CHAPTER ONE

A Thousand Plateaus in Context

Deleuze and Guattari burst onto the intellectual scene as collaborators with the first volume of *Capitalism and Schizophrenia*, entitled *Anti-Oedipus*, in 1972; the second volume, *A Thousand Plateaus*, followed eight years later. In between the two volumes of *Capitalism and Schizophrenia*, they co-authored *Kafka: Toward a Minor Literature*, whose importance for *A Thousand Plateaus* can hardly be exaggerated. Their last collaborative work, *What is Philosophy?*, appeared in 1991 (just before Guattari's death in 1992 and not long before Deleuze's suicide in 1995); among other things, it makes explicit the conception of philosophy they shared and had been practicing together for two decades. These other jointly-authored works provide important contexts for understanding *A Thousand Plateaus*, but so do their singly-authored works, particularly those of Deleuze. Although Deleuze was only five years older, he was a well-established philosopher when the two met in 1969, with many books to his credit and a growing reputation as one of the most important poststructuralist philosophers in France. Indeed, one of the things that attracted Guattari to Deleuze (for it was Guattari who proposed that they meet) was his command of western philosophy. Although Guattari had published just a few academic articles when they met (along with many more journalistic pieces), he was not only a star student and trainee of the reigning French psychoanalyst, Jacques Lacan, but co-director of one of the most radical psychiatric clinics in France, and also a militant political activist; it was Deleuze who suggested they work together. Each of them felt that the other could help them advance their work in ways they couldn't do alone, and the result was a unique and extraordinarily fertile collaboration that produced some of the most astonishing and important works of philosophy in the 20th century. After brief biographical sketches of the two authors, I will situate *A Thousand Plateaus* in its historical and philosophical contexts.

Gilles Deleuze

Born in 1925 to middle-class parents, Deleuze became enamored of literature and then philosophy in high school during WWII, and received his *agrégation* in philosophy in 1948. After teaching high school (*lycée*) for a number of years, he taught at the Sorbonne, held a position at the CNRS (National Center for Scientific Research) from 1960 until 1964, then returned to teaching at the University of Lyons until the completion of his doctorate in 1968, after which he was appointed to the faculty at the experimental University of Paris at Vincennes, where he taught (along with Michel Foucault, Guattari, and Lacan, among others) until he retired in 1987.

Starting in the late 1960s, Deleuze was, along with Jacques Derrida, the most important poststructuralist "philosopher of difference"—insisting that difference and becoming should have priority over identity and being, for reasons that I will examine in what follows. But whereas the younger Derrida's point of departure was existential phenomenology (Edmund Husserl, Martin Heidegger[1]), Deleuze shunned both existentialism and phenomenology for being too egocentric. Instead, Deleuze took his point of departure in readings of philosophers who were at the time not considered part of the mainstream: most notably Baruch Spinoza, Friedrich Nietzsche, and Henri Bergson.[2] It is probably fair to say that it was Deleuze who restored these maverick philosophers to importance within the field of French philosophy. This is particularly true of Nietzsche, whom Deleuze introduced into the realm of French letters with his book, *Nietzsche and Philosophy* in 1962. The signal exception to Deleuze's inclination to look off the beaten path for philosophical resources is Immanuel Kant, the most important of European Enlightenment philosophers: not only did Deleuze write a book on Kant, but Kant remained central to Deleuze's philosophical perspective throughout his career. Deleuze considered it his philosophical vocation to complete Kant's critical project by replacing the transcendental subject of all possible experience with the real genesis of our actual experience as a creative form of life—and a sketch of that genesis will be presented in Chapter 2. Karl Marx was another mainstream Western philosopher who was important to Deleuze, and he and Guattari insisted that they remained Marxists when most French poststructuralists were abandoning Marxism. Indeed, it appears that Deleuze was working on a book on "the greatness of Marx" (*Grandeur de Marx*) when he died. The other important thing to know about Deleuze is that, even though he considered himself a pure philosopher, he conducted important studies of "thought" in domains other than philosophy—most notably in literature, painting, and cinema—and drew for his philosophy on an extraordinary range of sources from outside of philosophy, including anthropology, mathematics, and complexity theory, as we will see.

Félix Guattari

Guattari's life-story was more checkered. Born in 1930, his family struggled with a number of business enterprises throughout his youth, several of which failed, and he was traumatized by witnessing the death of his grandfather. He was already politically active by the time WWII ended, and soon gave up the pharmacy studies recommended by his older brother to devote himself to political journalism and activism, and then to psychoanalytic training under Jacques Lacan. He soon became one of Lacan's most important students—but then left the Lacan orbit fairly early in his career, and became co-director with psychiatrist Jean Oury of the radical psychiatric clinic at La Borde. It is fair to say that, although Deleuze wrote extensively about psychoanalysis before meeting Guattari (especially in *Logic of Sense*), one of the main thrusts of *Anti-Oedipus* derives from the critique of Freud and Lacan developed by Guattari. In much the same way, it can be said that, although Deleuze had integrated Marx into his philosophical perspective before meeting Guattari (notably in *Difference and Repetition*), much of the critique of political economy and of capitalism in their first collaboration derives from Guattari and his experience as a militant Trotskyite in 1960s France. And indeed one way of understanding their first collaborative work, *Anti-Oedipus*, is as a combined political and philosophical reflection on the upheaval of May '68 in France—some of which was no doubt inspired by Deleuze's teaching at the radical Vincennes campus of the University of Paris, and some of which actually involved Guattari's militant activism.

Historical context

To say that the "events" or uprising or general strike of May '68 took most of France completely by surprise is perhaps an understatement, but both Deleuze and Guattari grew up during a time of radical political and social upheavals, including both the German Occupation and the French Resistance during WWII, as well as the economic rebuilding and modernization of France and the battle for Algerian liberation during the 1950s and 1960s. Jean-Paul Sartre's philosophy of political engagement was a decisive influence on both young men, although it expressed itself differently (in philosophy for Deleuze, in politics for Guattari). For a number of reasons, including both the active role of French communists in the Resistance and the rapid re-industrialization of France in the 1940s and 1950s, trade unions and the French Communist Party (PCF) remained an important presence in French politics and culture well into the 1980s, when *A Thousand Plateaus* appeared. And so engagements with Marx and Marxism—philosophical and/or political—were a necessary part of being a French intellectual or activist. Yet May 1968 took the French Communist Party more or less completely by surprise: workers themselves eventually joined the student cause (along with much of French society), but the trade unions only expressed support belatedly, and the PCF never did. Deleuze & Guattari's first collaboration, *Anti-Oedipus*, is often characterized as a result of the events of May '68, and as an attempt to account for them when no other political philosophy could—and this is indeed an apt characterization. But the collaboration proved longer-lasting than that. Three years after *Anti-Oedipus*, in 1975, their book on Kafka appeared, and a year after that, a long tract on the rhizome which would become the first plateau of *A Thousand Plateaus* four years later (1980). And although each of them continued to produce single-authored books while working together, their collaborative study *What is Philosophy?* (1991) was among the last major works either of them produced, Deleuze's *Essays Critical and Clinical* (1993), and Guattari's *Three Ecologies* (1989) and *Chaosmosis* (1992) notwithstanding.

Philosophical contexts

To their first collaboration (*Anti-Oedipus*), Deleuze brings a whole set of conceptual resources derived from Spinoza, Leibniz, Hume, Kant, Nietzsche, Bergson, and Jung, just as Guattari brings to the collaboration a set of invaluable resources derived from Marx, Hjelmslev and Lacan.[3] From his readings of Hume, Nietzsche, Bergson and Jung, Deleuze had, well before seriously confronting psychoanalysis, already developed a philosophical concept of the unconscious that combined instinct (from Hume and Jung), *élan vital* (from Bergson) and will-to-power (from Nietzsche) with an insistence that the unconscious is accessible only in and through its contingent expression in historical institutions and archetypes. Instincts and institutions are so inextricably mixed that instinct never appears in and of itself; and at the same time, any instinct can express itself in a variety of institutional forms. Ultimately, individual psychotherapy becomes indistinguishable—and inseparable—from institutional and social reform (as Guattari was insisting for reasons of his own at the La Borde clinic). The primary aim of *Anti-Oedipus*, and part of the project of fulfilling the promise of Kantian critique, was to replace Freudian (and Lacanian) psychoanalysis with a "revolutionary materialist psychiatry" called schizoanalysis; and for schizoanalysis, the unconscious is not structured like a language (as it was according to Lacan), but is rather the locus of a single vital desiring-energy formerly known as will-to-power, labor-power, and libido. It is due to Christianity and capitalism that this vital energy gets divided in three and all too often turned against itself, which leads to Deleuze & Guattari's call to simultaneously free creativity from other-worldly asceticism and an overly-narrow scientific reality-principle (following Nietzsche), free labor-power from its exploitation by capital (following Marx), and free libidinal desire from Oedipal repression (following Freud).

Schizoanalysis advances the Kantian project in three principal ways, and ends up merging it with those of Marx and Nietzsche. In making the object of critique the real genesis of our actual experience rather than the conditions of all possible experience, Deleuze & Guattari transform Kant's syntheses of the understanding into passive syntheses of the unconscious. Based on his so-called "Copernican revolution" in epistemology,[4] and speaking in the name of reason, Kant had asserted that the conscious mind utilizes a specific set of processes (which he called the "syntheses of apprehension, reproduction, and recognition") to arrive at knowledge, and had insisted furthermore that knowledge would have to conform to these processes or else stand condemned as illegitimate. Of crucial importance for Kant was the idea that, since these processes were **constitutive** of conscious thought, they provided **immanent** criteria for judging knowledge as valid or invalid, depending on whether it was based on legitimate or illegitimate use of the three syntheses. In a similar way, but speaking not in the name of reason but in the name of desire and especially schizophrenic desire, Deleuze & Guattari insist that the unconscious operates according to a specific set of syntheses to process or constitute experience, and that psychoanalysis must either be shown to conform to these processes or else stand condemned as invalid. While this first transformation renders the syntheses passive and unconscious, a second transformation shifts the locus of the unconscious from the individual subject to the historically specific groups and social formations to which a given subject belongs. The unconscious thereby becomes something like a "collective unconscious"—but one that is specific to historically-situated groups and institutions rather than eternal or universal. The result, finally, is that critique becomes fully social rather than just epistemological: ultimately, schizoanalysis condemns psychoanalysis as a reflection or projection of capitalism; as a historical materialist psychiatry, schizoanalysis will call not just for psychoanalytic doctrine, but for social relations in general, to conform to the syntheses of the unconscious. Schizoanalysis is thus revolutionary in a Marxist sense, whereas psychoanalysis is not. Yet here Deleuze & Guattari's Marxist analyses acquire a distinctly Nietzschean foundation: the social ideal is not what best represents the interests of the proletariat (or humanity as a whole), but what **least** contradicts the "logic" of the unconscious and the bodily forces animating its syntheses; revolutionary society, too, will have to conform to these unconscious processes or else stand condemned as repressive.

In *Anti-Oedipus*, the link between labor-power and libido is forged through the deployment of two terms: desiring-production and territorialization. The hyphenated term practically speaks for itself: desiring-production encompasses both labor-power and libido, and Deleuze & Guattari's historical analyses in *Anti-Oedipus* show that it is under capitalism that the two are most completely separated from one another. The terms territorialization, de-territorialization, and re-territorialization link psychoanalysis and political economy by designating the investment of energy in specific areas of the body and the economy, the withdrawal of such investments, and their re-investment elsewhere. By the time they wrote *A Thousand Plateaus*, however, these terms converge with the terms stratification and de-stratification, and have a far wider scope of reference, as we will see, characterizing processes at work throughout the cosmos.

But in *Anti-Oedipus*, territorialization is accompanied by processes of coding, de-coding and re-coding, which help guide the investment of energy. Thus the act of marrying may de-code a young man of his status of eligible bachelor, and re-code him as off-limits for the investment of others' desires; advertising, in a similar way, guides consumer tastes and purchases by de-coding last year's styles and re-coding this year's as "in fashion." Capitalist society is distinctive, according to Deleuze & Guattari, in that it is based on markets, and therefore de-codes—"strips of its halo" as Marx and Engels had put it in *The Communist Manifesto*—everything that had intrinsic value and replaces it with strictly quantitative, monetary value. The process of commodification contributes to exploitation, to be sure, but it also frees desire from capture in social codes, thereby releasing huge amounts of free-flowing energy that capital cannot always re-capture for the sake of private accumulation. Deleuze & Guattari thus claim that what they call "schizophrenia"—by which they mean not a mental illness, but the absolutely free, de-coded flow of desire—is the limit of capitalism, albeit a limit that capital continually displaces by re-capturing schizophrenic flows as best it can, whether in commodities, institutional norms, or as a last resort in asylums. They are careful to insist that schizophrenia is a limit because desire never appears in absolutely pure form, any more than instinct does: it is always inevitably expressed through codes and institutions, even if these codes and institutions are always contingent, historically variable, and therefore susceptible to change.

Deleuze's magnum opus, *Difference and Repetition*, provides important tools for assessing the intensity of freedom of variation expressed in a given codification or institutionalization of desire: it is always a question of the degree of difference involved in repetition. Strict instinctual determination of behavior (as is the case with many insects, where a given stimulus inevitably triggers the same response) involves repetition without any difference whatsoever, or what Deleuze calls "bare repetition." Humans are not instinctually determined in that way, as I have said, but habits and neuroses nonetheless produce a kind of bare repetition in human behavior, for better and for worse: the bare repetition of habit can save us the trouble of thinking through everything we do every time, but there are also bad habits; neurosis is a form of bare repetition more or less completely beyond our control, an especially bad habit that may require therapy to break. In philosophy, privileging identity over difference, fixed Being over fluid becoming, can be likened to a form of neurosis, inasmuch as Being constrains repetition to operate with a minimum of difference, and subordinates what already is different or could become different to what is always the same. Creative repetition, by contrast, promotes difference over identity, and the greater the degree of difference in repetition, the freer human behavior can become—with schizophrenia designating the absolute upper limit of freedom.

For example, learning to play a musical instrument involves a significant amount of bare repetition—such as practicing scales. Once a certain level of proficiency is reached, a piece of classical music can be played from a pre-composed score; this also involves a significant degree of bare repetition, since a composed piece is supposed to be performed more or less the same way every time, with only a small degree of "expressive freedom" allowed to the performer. Once another critical threshold of proficiency is reached, however, improvisation becomes possible, and here the ratio of difference to repetition increases exponentially, so that creative repetition replaces bare repetition. Jazz musicians will take a familiar tune, and de-code it by playing it a different way each time—sometimes to the point of making the once-familiar tune almost unrecognizable. So-called "free jazz" goes so far as to improvise without starting from a familiar tune in the first place—thereby coming that much closer to the outer limit of schizophrenia. In *A Thousand Plateaus*, the term "de-territorialization" tends to replace schizophrenia: jazz musicians de-territorialize a tune by improvising on or around it. What Deleuze & Guattari call **relative** de-territorialization entails improvising on a familiar tune's chord sequence (or "chord chart") in a specific key. To adapt the language of complexity theory, the musical key represents a "basin of attraction" specifying which notes and chords (such as the tonic, dominant, and sub-dominant, the minor seventh and minor third) serve as "attractors" around which the improvisation will take place. But it can also happen that jazz musicians will unexpectedly change keys, or indeed suddenly switch from one tune to a completely different one (with its own chord sequence)—that is to say, change basins of attraction—in the middle of an improvisation: these are instances of **absolute** de-territorialization. Free jazz, operating at the extreme without chord charts and even without respect to recognizable key signatures, is an instance of continuous absolute de-territorialization, a creative line of flight. The challenge of improvisation, in such circumstances, is to maximize the degrees of difference in repetition, to maximize the absolute de-territorialization of a song, while nevertheless maintaining its **consistency** as a piece of music. Indeed, maintaining or creating **consistency** without imposing unity, identity, or organization—without resorting to bare repetition of the same—might be said to constitute the holy grail of all of Deleuze & Guattari's work, in ethics and politics as well as aesthetics. While they acknowledge the advantages of habit and the importance of institutions, both of which constrain the degree of difference in repetition, their ideal is to maximize difference and to experiment with variation, to leave the comfort-zone of home on the thread of a tune, as they put it [311], in order to improvise with the world, as we will see.

Within a few years the publication of *Anti-Oedipus*, three important texts appear: they include the two collaboratively-written works—*Kafka: Toward a Minor Literature* (1975) and *Rhizome* (1976)—and a new edition (the third) of Deleuze's study of *Proust and Signs* (1976), which, like the second edition (of 1970), shows the increasing influence of Guattari on Deleuze's thought. Reserving discussion of the Rhizome plateau for later, I will outline here what the two literary studies, of Proust and Kafka, contribute to the writing of *A Thousand Plateaus*. From both authors, Deleuze & Guattari extract an image of thought that, by repeating it with a difference, they will make their own; thus, to a certain extent, all three of Deleuze & Guattari's works from the mid–1970s contribute to the rhizome as the image of thought that opens, and might even be said to inform, *A Thousand Plateaus*.

Throughout his magnum opus, *In Search of Lost Time*, Proust emphasizes the importance of involuntary memory: images of the past that occur to us involuntarily are far more important than memories that are recollected at will. A certain sensation in the present will suddenly evoke a memory from the past, without there being any direct or immediately obvious connection between the two, and without involving any conscious intention whatsoever. These memories are far richer and reveal more about the past than voluntary memory can, yet they defy conscious mastery. This makes the project of retrieving lost time a difficult, if not impossible, task. As the novel unfolds, a vast network of connections between times past and times present emerges, over which the narrator tries to exert some measure of control, or from which at least he will try to distill some kind of meaning. But the longer Deleuze works with Guattari—the first edition of *Proust and Signs* (1960) was written before they met; the second edition (1970) appeared as they were writing *Anti-Oedipus* together; the third and final edition appeared the same year as *Rhizome* (1976)—the less he sides with the narrator or the project of retrieving lost time, and the more he highlights the writing-machine that produces the network of "involuntary" temporal connections to begin with. Whereas Kant had insisted on **adding** the subjective "I" to experience, in order to provide a stable, coherent ground for true knowledge and ethical action, Proust leads Deleuze in the opposite direction, by **subtracting** the subject from experience, and treating the subject as a by-product or residue of experience itself. From this perspective, what is paramount in Proust's work is the patchwork of temporal relations woven by the narrative machine which produces the impression of "a life"—and the question of whether the narrator can ever take complete control of that life becomes secondary. Such a life is an open temporal **multiplicity**; that is to say, it consists precisely and only of the connections composing the patchwork. Its possible or projected unification at the command or as the property of the narrator (or author) then appears as a supplementary dimension added to the patchwork-life (or the novel), but not necessary for it to maintain its **consistency** as "a" life. This insistence on consistency affords a contrast not just with Kant, but with Heidegger as well: for where the latter emphasizes ex-istence—and to ex-ist is to stand out, for Heidegger—Deleuze & Guattari emphasize consistency—where to con-sist entails being-with rather than standing-out: togetherness, the multiple logics of "and" and "with" rather than the singular logic of being. In any case, it is the special para-personal **consistency** of the Proustian literary machine that Deleuze & Guattari will adapt for *A Thousand Plateaus*: the book will consist of a patchwork of relations among concepts and plateaus, intentionally not unified by a single line of argument, authorial voice or disciplinary perspective—an intention made all the easier to realize inasmuch as they are writing as co-authors, one a philosopher and the other a militant anti-psychiatrist and political activist. Deleuze even suggested on one occasion (*Dialogues II*, p. 17) that he and Guattari didn't share a common understanding of one of their central concepts: the "Body-without-Organs."

Even more explicitly than Deleuze's study of Proust's literary machine, the collaborative study of Kafka will produce the rhizome as an image of thought: from the very first page, Kafka's work is characterized as a "rhizome, or a burrow [*terrier*]" [K 3], just as *A Thousand Plateaus* will be characterized as a rhizome, from its very first plateau. In the world Kafka depicts, every room is connected to innumerable other rooms, by means of doors and passageways, some of them hidden or subterranean. Any room, it seems, can connect with any other, depending on circumstances. Particularly in the novels, the arrangement of space in Kafka is like a cross between a bureaucratic organizational chart showing lines of power or desire and a blueprint or roadmap showing the actual (fictional) locations of buildings and offices within them; more like an organizational chart, though, the connecting lines can change at any time, for unknown reasons, as relations of power and desire themselves change. Where Proust's patchwork was a temporal multiplicity, Kafka's rhizome is more of a spatial multiplicity. *A Thousand Plateaus*, too, should be understood as a spatial multiplicity, with innumerable passageways connecting various concepts and examples beneath the unavoidably linear arrangement of words forming sentences, sentences forming paragraphs, and so forth. If, as Deleuze announces in the Preface to *Difference and Repetition*, philosophy should come more and more to resemble science fiction, there is an important sense in which *A Thousand Plateaus* fits the bill: the text is to a great degree modeled on images of thought coming from the realm of fiction (Proust and Kafka), at the same time that it also draws heavily, as we will see, on the findings of contemporary mathematics and science.

Before turning to an overview of the book in the next chapter, however, a few words should be said about Deleuze & Guattari's subsequent and last collaboration, entitled *What is Philosophy?* (1991). In much the same way that *Rhizome* might be considered a theoretical re-statement of the image of thought developed in the preceding book on Kafka, *What is Philosophy?* can be considered a theoretical re-statement of the philosophy developed in the preceding *A Thousand Plateaus*. In other words, the later work can be considered a kind of summary and clarification of what they were doing in what remains to this day their most important collaborative work. And because *A Thousand Plateaus* draws so heavily on science and literature, as I have just suggested, one of the important contributions of the later book is to draw clear distinctions between philosophy and science and between philosophy and the arts. Thought is not the exclusive privilege of philosophy, Deleuze & Guattari recognize, and indeed they borrow freely from thought produced in a wide range of disciplines (by no means limited to science and literature). Of particular importance, as I will show in Chapter 2, is the inverse relationship between the domains of the **virtual** and the **actual** in science and philosophy. Throughout Deleuze's work, the domain of the virtual is said to be composed of Problems which it is the task of philosophy to articulate as cogently as possible, while the domain of the actual is comprised of a variety of contingent Solutions to those Problems—and these terms will be capitalized in what follows whenever they are being used in this specific philosophical sense. (The same will be true for the terms "State," "Despot," "Being," "Event," "Life," "Face" and "Significant" when they are used in a specifically philosophical sense.) While it is true that some Problems can be said to arise within philosophy itself, Deleuze & Guattari insisted strenuously that philosophy needs to keep in touch with all that lies outside it, including not just political situations, but also the most recent developments in science—and it is there that our overview will begin.

CHAPTER TWO

Overview of Themes

PRELUDE

A Thousand Plateaus is an unusual book. It was written as a rhizome, Deleuze & Guattari say. So it's more like a patchwork quilt than a piece of fabric, which can only develop in one direction—left to right, let us say—and must stay within the boundaries set on the top and bottom edges, as it were, by a single discipline. Instead, the book's arguments (of which there are many) go off in all directions, intervene in debates in all kinds of disciplines and are therefore more like patches added haphazardly to a patchwork quilt. The fact that such a quilt does not have to take the shape of a rectangle or a square, but can become totally lopsided and develop in any direction or many directions, doesn't mean that there can't be colors or textures that repeat here and there, creating patterns: the book definitely has conceptual motifs or refrains flowing through it, resurfacing here and there in sometimes slightly different forms or terms, only to re-submerge and then reappear elsewhere. In this respect, the book could be said to resemble a musical score; and it is true that music occupies a special place in Deleuze & Guattari's conceptual repertoire. But it is more than that: music expresses the highest coefficient of de-territorialization of any medium in the universe, while at the same time the dynamics of the universe itself can be understood as a kind of music—the so-called "music of the spheres" being perhaps the least of it. A musical score, however, bears too great a resemblance to a piece of fabric to serve as an adequate image of thought for **this** book: like fabric, a musical score, too, is bounded on the top and bottom edges, so to speak, by the number of instruments in the orchestra, and it unfolds in only one direction (from left to right). So I prefer to think of the book along the lines of a chord chart, of the kind jazz musicians use to improvise by. This image has disadvantages of its own: a chord chart still implies a linear progression of chords serving as common scaffolding for the musicians' contributions, and *A Thousand Plateaus* is emphatically **not** linear, as we shall see. Deleuze & Guattari indeed say that the plateaus of which the book is composed may be read in any order whatsoever. Any single reading of the entire book, however—provided that the **whole** book does indeed get read, as is the intention here—will arguably produce something of a linear reading, in much the same way that improvising from a chord chart will on any single occasion produce one linear performance of it among many possible performances. That having been said, we are ready to launch forth on the thread of a tune to improvise with *A Thousand Plateaus*, and the performance that follows should be understood as "a" reading of it, one among many possible readings, intended not to distill its meaning but to perform and explicate some of its potential.

Philosophical background

A Thousand Plateaus is best understood as providing the metaphysics appropriate to contemporary science—a science based on non-linear mathematics, and sometimes referred to as complexity theory or dynamic systems theory—in much the same way that Kant provided a metaphysics appropriate to the science of his day, Newtonian physics. "One must make metaphysics into the correlate for modern science," Deleuze once said, "exactly as modern science is the correlate of a potential metaphysics"—and this is precisely the metaphysics laid out in *A Thousand Plateaus*.[1] Among other things, this metaphysics will address questions of epistemology, ontology, anthropology, ethics, and politics—and the five sections of the next chapter ("Reading the Text") will outline the interventions the book makes in each of these fields in turn. But first, some philosophical background is necessary against which to situate the contributions of *A Thousand Plateaus* as a whole.

Probably the most important difference between Deleuze & Guattari's philosophy and Kant's has to do with their respective conceptions of time: for Kant it was linear and reversible, while for Deleuze & Guattari, and for most state-of-the-art science, it is non-linear and irreversible. Reversible, linear time corresponds to the mechanistic, calculable view of the universe made famous by Newton: two billiard balls on a collision course always interact the same way, and if you could rewind and replay the interaction 100 times, the billiard balls would take the same trajectories every time. Start the process of evolution over 100 times, however, and you would get up to 100 different results: this is an example of the difference between linear-mechanistic causality and non-linear, emergent causality; the latter involves singularities or bifurcation-points, and it is particularly at these undecidable points that time reveals itself to be irreversible.

Deleuze's philosophy of time

Here we need to take a closer look at Deleuze's philosophy of time. In his *magnum opus*, *Difference and Repetition*, Deleuze presents a view of time in terms of what he calls three passive syntheses—those of present, past, and future. As I said in Chapter One, Deleuze considers these time-binding syntheses to be strictly passive because of his concern to avoid the ego-centrism (or the "transcendental subjectivism") of much of modern philosophy, from Descartes and Kant up through phenomenology: the syntheses of time are not the operations of an active, transcendental self that manages or processes its experience, they are passive operations which in fact give rise to all experience in the first place, including our experience of the self.

These syntheses have been described as a "phenomenology of the present," an "ontology of the past," and a "pragmatics of the future"—which is a good start.[2] It might be said that "phenomenology" is a rather curious choice for the synthesis of the present, since Deleuze rejected phenomenology because of its transcendental subjectivism, but I think the choice is tenable in this particular sense: Deleuze's account of the temporal syntheses in *Difference and Repetition* seems to take as its point of departure the way we experience time, and deduces from that the way the syntheses must operate.

The conventional, linear depiction of time—at least as old as Newton, with philosophical roots reaching as far back as

Aristotle—presents it as a straight line in which each passing moment recedes behind the present, just as each approaching moment arrives from a future stretched out in front of us along the time-line we are traveling. It is surprising how pervasive and apparently convincing this depiction is at first blush—given that it is simply not true to our experience of time at all. For the past exists for us as a whole, not strung out along a line: to retrieve a past moment from six weeks ago, we don't have to rewind the entire chain of events to get there: we jump immediately to the last days of summer. And we can jump from there to any other past moments, without having to trace out or locate those moments on any linear time-lines. The past is, if you will, omni-present to itself. At least that's the way it seems to us.

But then the question becomes: is this true only of our experience of the past?—or is it true of the past itself? In other words, how do you get from phenomenology (or how things appear) to ontology and how things actually are? To be sure, past events co-exist in memory—we can scan the past and access this event or jump to that event, without having to replay the entire succession of moments between them. But how do we get from this psychological experience/recollection of the past to the notion that past events themselves co-exist ontologically?

This is where Deleuze draws on Henri Bergson. The past for Bergson is not the repository of a linear series of passing presents, but an a-temporal bloc where each and every past event co-exists with all the others. For Bergson, it is not just in memory that one event can be connected with any other, irrespective of their respective places on a time-line: in the Bergsonian past, past events themselves co-exist, inhabiting a realm that Bergson calls the virtual: the past as a virtual whole (or as a bloc) is the condition for actual events to take place in the present, just as—for example— the language-system as a virtual whole (or what the structuralists call a structure, *langue*) is the condition for actual speech acts to take place in the present. This view of the past as a condition for the actualization of the present connects with the privileging of becoming over being that Deleuze adopts from Friedrich Nietzsche. Being is merely a momentary, subsidiary, and largely illusory suspension (or "contraction") of becoming, according to this view; becoming is always primary and fundamental. This means not merely that each and every thing **has** a history—rather, each and every thing simply **is** its history: apparent being is always the temporary but actual culmination or expression of real becoming; it is the present actualization of antecedent conditions contained in the virtual past. In the terminology of *A Thousand Plateaus*, the process of actualization is called "stratification."

But to say that any entity is "its" history isn't quite right either: each entity or state of affairs is not just its own self-contained history, but in fact an expression of the history of the entire cosmos, an expression of the entire past contracted via passive synthesis (as Deleuze puts it) from the perspective of that present thing. This philosophical view aligns directly with contemporary science as informed by non-linear mathematics and complexity theory: basins or islands of linear determinacy certainly exist in the cosmos, but they emerge from a vast sea of non-linear dynamics. Determinate being does emerge occasionally from becoming, but it arises always from a broader context of non-linear indeterminacy. Therefore—and this is crucial—the determination of every actual being by the virtual past in its entirety remains **contingent** for Deleuze: it only has determinacy when read retroactively; it could always have happened otherwise. That is why a process like evolution can only be studied retroactively, and why repeating evolution one hundred times could produce up to one hundred different results.

Here it becomes important to understand the relations between science and Deleuze & Guattari's practice and conception of philosophy, especially since, as I and they have said, their philosophy is presented as a correlate of contemporary, non-linear science. The aim of science is to narrow down any thing's antecedent conditions to the point where virtual becomings succumb to actual being and the thing appears to obey the eternal "laws of nature"; philosophy, by contrast, retains the complexity and non-linearity of antecedent conditions, so that a thing's present being is understood as a more or less temporary and unstable contraction of its becomings. In this respect (and here I am jumping ahead to categorical distinctions that only become explicit in *What is Philosophy?*), the relations between the virtual and the actual in science and in philosophy are the obverse of one another. Entities and states of affairs come into being when a set of virtual conditions actually gets expressed in a specific way. By controlling variables and repeating experiments, science focuses squarely on actualized being, turning its back on virtuality to define actuality as accurately as possible. Philosophy, by contrast, moves in the reverse direction: philosophy turns away from a given state of affairs toward the virtual conditions from which it emerged. The task of philosophy is to extract from a state of affairs a map of the virtual of which it is an actualization—for any state of affairs is but one among many potential actualizations of its virtual conditions. The virtual is always richer in potential than the actual. In the terminology of *A Thousand Plateaus*, the virtual realm is called "the plane of consistency."

It should be said that this stark contrast between science and philosophy is ultimately too schematic. Contemporary sciences, the sciences informed by non-linear mathematics and complexity theory, are able to take into account a far greater portion of the intensive processes of becoming than, say, Newtonian mechanics ever did. This is one reason why the interplay between contemporary math and science and philosophy is so fruitful in Deleuze & Guattari. Yet even if it is true that science and philosophy share more than ever an interest in becoming, the aims of the two endeavors are nevertheless quite distinct: one is to denote actual reality as accurately as possible (including the intensive processes that generate that actuality), and the other is to map virtual potential as suggestively or productively as possible. So the task of philosophy can be defined not simply as the creation of concepts, but more precisely as the extraction of concepts from actual states of affairs. Philosophy both depends on science for an accurate account of states of affairs, yet also departs from science in its aim to map the real virtual potential of actual states of affairs.

On the basis of this understanding of the past as the virtual repository of multiple potentials and the present as one actualization of such potentials among many, the third synthesis of time, the future, appears as the unforeseeable selection, from among the inexhaustible set of virtual conditions, of one sub-set of conditions that will become relevant through subsequent actualization. Not only is the present only one actualization among many, but its relation to the past is not exhausted or determined in its actualization alone: its relation to the past will have been determined by future actualizations, each of which successively alters the relations between that present and its relevant pasts. This synthesis can be considered a pragmatics of the future because, to invoke a key term from *Anti-Oedipus*, desire is a force that scans the past from the perspective of the present in search of possible combinations to actualize. And philosophy, as I have said, is an explicit mode of such a pragmatics: it scans the virtual realm from within a problematic actual state of affairs in order to map its potential to become otherwise, in order to re-submerge inert islands of apparent being in the oceanic flux of becomings with a view to actualizing something else, something different, something better. In this way, a new, non-linear conception of time ends up suggesting a quite novel role for philosophy, compared with older, more conventional views of linear time.

A self-organizing chaosmos

One key result of this difference is that for Deleuze & Guattari, the cosmos is self-organizing, whereas for Kant it had to obey laws. The idea that order could increase rather than decrease over time may seem to contradict the second law of thermodynamics—the law of entropy—but this law presupposes that the universe forms a closed system; it does not apply in an open system with positive net inputs of energy. Since Deleuze & Guattari view the cosmos precisely as an open system, its tendency toward self-organization was taken as a given—and was in addition readily observable in the evolution of life on earth, an open system with very clear positive net energy gain, coming in this case from the sun. So where Kant replaced God with Man, Deleuze & Guattari replace Man with Life, and beyond Life, with a self-organizing "chaosmos" [cosmos + chaos] whose modes of organization emerge from matter immanently instead of being imposed from above as form or law.

Deleuze and Guattari will call the sum total of all virtual potential in the chaosmos "the plane of consistency." It is composed of potential Problems, and the process of actualization proposes, expresses, or experiments with various Solutions to those problems. In this context, it can be helpful to compare virtual problems with structuralist structures and the notion of "immanent causality" developed by French Marxist philosopher Louis Althusser (whose early work influenced Deleuze, and whose later work was in turn influenced by Deleuze). For example, the language-system is a virtual structure, from which speech-acts emerge; each speech-act expresses or actualizes a certain potential within the language-system, yet without ever exhausting the system's total potential. These speech-acts are conditioned (in a structuralist sense) by the language-system, but are not caused (in any mechanistic, linear sense) by it. Like language, the cosmos is an open (non-linear) system, and so there is never just one Solution to a given Problem: the virtual field of becoming is always richer than the solutions that get actualized. But even if the virtual field of the chaosmos is infinite, it is not indeterminate, for if it were, both science and philosophy would be impossible: there is infinite potential for becoming to actualize itself in different beings, but only and always within the parameters immanent to this universe as we know it, with its specific constants such as the speed of light, the gravitational constant, and so on. (In a similar way, the number of potential grammatical sentences in English is infinite, but not indeterminate: sentences are grammatical only and always within the parameters set by the rules of English grammar, and there is a whole set of word combinations that are thereby excluded.) Operating with these constants or constraints, matter can "solve" its Problems by self-organizing in an infinite number of ways, but always in determinate forms or modes. We can see here the sense in which Deleuze's ontology relies on science to furnish some of the determinations of becoming that give rise to the self-organization of being.

This notion of the immanent or emergent self-organization of matter is central to Deleuze & Guattari's metaphysics, and among the most important and widespread of these modes of self-organization (which they refer to as "abstract machines") are intertwined processes of differentiation and consolidation—processes which can explain the development of the universe as well as the evolution of Life, as we will see. Hence the emphasis on "abstract" in abstract machines: these are processes at work in many different kinds of matter. The actualization of these abstract machines in different kinds of matter produces two other types of machine: concrete machinic assemblages and collective assemblages of enunciation (which correspond quite closely to what French philosopher and intellectual historian Michel Foucault called "practices" and "discourses"); these two types of machine interact to form different strata. In *A Thousand Plateaus*, Deleuze and Guattari divide the chaosmos into three major sectors that I will call "mega-strata": the inorganic, the organic and the alloplastic.

As a first approximation—but only an approximation—we can think of these mega-strata as corresponding to matter, Life, and culture respectively. I will start with the inorganic stratum, then move on to Life, and then to culture.

The inorganic stratum

The inorganic stratum starts with a bang—with the Big Bang, that is (or the Big Pulse, as some scientists now prefer to say). A mass of plasma streams forth that is at first completely homogeneous (that is to say, undifferentiated), but where plasma flows start to swerve and form eddies, differences emerge, leading to the consolidation of the first elements and eventually the formation of stars. This is the first instance of the processes of expansion and contraction, differentiation and consolidation, that Deleuze & Guattari will show to operate throughout the cosmos—and for which they sometimes borrow the terms "systolic" and "diastolic" (as if the cosmos had a heartbeat and blood flows). Further contractions within the gravitational pressure-cooker of stars lead to the differentiation and consolidation of additional chemical elements (eventually including carbon), while gravitational contraction at a vastly different scale also propels the emergence of galaxies and solar systems. Thus a galactic stratum emerges from the basic processes of chaosmosis, and from the galactic stratum eventually emerges a solar system, and within it a geological stratum, and from there, the differentiation of organic from inorganic chemistry and eventually the emergence of carbon-based life. And so at the speed of thought, we reach in a matter of seconds the organic stratum which actually took eons to develop. The apparently chaotic dating of the plateaus in *A Thousand Plateaus*—one plateau dated in the thousands of years BC, another in terms of a single day in November of a specific year—is no doubt intended to reflect the vastly disparate timescales in which these processes play themselves out: evolutionary time is far more rapid than geological time, and cultural time is faster yet, as we shall see—outpaced only by the theoretically infinite speed of philosophical thought itself.

The organic stratum

Turning now to the organic stratum, the major diastolic and systolic processes of self-organization here are conventionally known as random genetic mutation and natural or ecological selection. Mutation produces differences, and selection consolidates those differences into discrete organs and species. Here in the organic stratum it seems obvious that Life responds to Problems by experimenting with different kinds of Solutions—such as the Problem of how light-sensitivity can contribute to nutrient uptake, to which eyes and chlorophyll, for example, are two very different kinds of Solution. But in retrospect, chaosmosis has always involved finding solutions to various problems: mountains, for example, are one Solution to the problem of tectonic pressure; and diamonds are another. It's just that Life experiments more rapidly, differentiates more flamboyantly, runs through failures and successes more dramatically, and involves Problems the human life-form can more easily recognize as similar if not identical to some of its own—most notably the Problem called "survival." Due to differences in time-scale and speed, we may find it hard to identify with a rock's struggle to survive (although it, too, is bound to die, in its own way), whereas the survival struggles of other mammals and even of plants often strike a chord in us. In any case, within the organic stratum, survival—both for species and for individuals—is a central Problem, to which evolution throws up innumerable Solutions, some of which fail, while others prevail (at least for a time). Evolution has no pre-ordained course: taking place in and as an open system, it operates according to a process of what is called "probe-head" experimentation, with life-forms arising haphazardly from random mutation and then experimenting with different organic structures and behavioral repertoires to see whether they can survive within a given ecological milieu. And in this way, Life is constantly self-expanding, filling as many ecological niches as possible to the maximum degree possible—that is, to the degree allowed by the continuing survival of other ecologically related species and the constraints of the eco-system, the biosphere, and the chaosmos as we know it.

So we can say that, within the region of the plane of consistency known as the organic stratum, survival is Life's principal Problem, and that evolution experiments with myriad Solutions to it. But then a critical threshold within the organic stratum is reached: some species start addressing the Problem of survival by self-organizing socially. I will call this the "Intra-Species Social Organization" Problem (the ISSO Problem)—and it is worth singling out not principally because the human life-form itself addresses and experiments with Solutions to the Problem, but because of the number of other, very different species that also address the Problem, and do so in instructively different ways—but also in instructively **similar** ways. Insects, for example, self-organize socially on the basis of rigid morpho-genetic differences and inexorable chemical signals—very differently from us (until you factor in the role of pheromones in human sexual attraction and mating). Cattle self-organize socially in herds, while wolves self-organize socially in packs—each species operating according to very different principles, degrees of role differentiation, mechanisms of coordination, and so forth. To what extent do humans organize socially like herd animals, such as cattle?—as Nietzsche might ask. To what extent do humans organize socially in packs, the way wolves do?—as Deleuze & Guattari themselves ask. Birds self-organize socially by singing songs and marking territories, but they also do so by flocking. What do national anthems and commercial markets as modes of human social organization have to do with these avian social behaviors? How closely do national anthems resemble the territorial songs of birds? And in what sense do market behaviors resemble those of flocks of birds or schools of fish? What degree, if any, of insect social organization remains effective in humans? Is human social organization ultimately closer to that of cattle or that of wolves? Are we a herd animal or a pack animal? And if, as is most likely, we are neither one alone, what kind of combination or mixture might we be? Which of our behavior patterns more closely resembles herd behavior, and which ones resemble pack behavior?

But we are getting ahead of ourselves (a recurring problem with the speed of thought): with wolves, we have already crossed a second key threshold within the organic stratum, where species learning or Problem-solving gives rise to individual learning. Through the intertwined processes of differentiating mutation and consolidating speciation, evolution as a whole learns its lessons by experimenting with different life-forms, some of which succeed while others fail. But then in some social species (such as wolves), learning devolves to individuals **within** the species. This is not true of insects: they may gather and communicate information (chemically), but they do not learn social roles: insects' roles are programmed ontogenetically. Wolf cubs, by contrast, learn social skills and roles within the pack by playing around with a relatively large repertoire of behaviors, from which a certain set get selected and eventually determine the socially-differentiated role a given cub will then play in the pack. Life's experimentation on the scale of entire species gives rise to play-based experimentation on the scale of individuals within the species. And here, I want to suggest, philosophy is not far behind: where wolf cubs experiment with social roles in play, philosophers experiment with what Deleuze & Guattari will (in *What is Philosophy?*) call "conceptual personae" in thought. We philosophize as wolves (**not** as cattle). Yet we also have to ask: what language-games **do** we play as cattle? (Electoral rhetoric comes to mind as one such game, and advertising as another.) But we are getting ahead of ourselves, again. For we have, almost imperceptibly, crossed into the alloplastic or cultural stratum.

The alloplastic stratum

I say "almost imperceptibly" because drawing a boundary-line between the organic and alloplastic strata is difficult—and furthermore, it does not correspond to the distinction between animal and human. Bird songs are not genetically or instinctually programmed: they vary regionally within the same species, and therefore can be considered as cultural as anything human. "Art does not wait for humans to begin," Deleuze & Guattari famously say somewhere in *A Thousand Plateaus* [320]. And as I have already suggested, many of what may appear to be distinctly human Solutions to the Intra-Species Social Organization Problem have approximate equivalents in other life forms. Many, many animals—not just birds—mark and defend their territory; and in much the same way, humans living in tribes and in nation states alike mark and defend their territory. Similarly, just as there are herd and pack Solutions to the ISSO Problem among some animals, there are sedentary and nomadic Solutions to the human

ISSO Problem, which Deleuze & Guattari discuss in terms of the sedentary State-form and the nomadic war-machine. Then again, markets represent another Solution to the human ISSO problem, a Solution resembling the flocking behavior of birds, inasmuch as markets foster a gradually increasing division and articulation of labor—a gradual increase, that is, until the advent of capitalism, which catalyzes and accelerates the division/articulation of labor dramatically. Ultimately, what distinguishes the human element of these various kinds of Solution is that human social organization passes through the Symbolic order of representation—that is to say, through the symbol-systems of language, symbols and money. And it is here, with the Symbolic treatment of the plane of consistency, that posing Problems and experimenting with Solutions reaches its maximum speed and extension.

But there is another distinctive feature of the way humans address the Problem of survival compared to the ways other animals (and plants) do: humans actively **produce** their means of life in ways that few other animals do, in a historical variety of what Marxists call modes of production. Deleuze & Guattari call the cultural mega-stratum the "alloplastic" stratum partly in order to highlight the fact that humans (along with just a few other species, to a lesser degree) actively shape their environment, rather than merely consuming what the environment has to offer (the way most species do). Yet Deleuze & Guattari pose the relation between economic production and other aspects of social life in terms very different from the base-superstructure model of orthodox Marxism; they pose it in terms of virtual Problems and actual Solutions. Deleuze says in *Difference and Repetition*,

> In all rigor, there are only economic social problems, even though the solutions may be juridical, political, or ideological, and the problems may be **expressed** in those fields of resolvability.... That is why 'the economic' [instance] is never given properly speaking, but rather designates a differential virtuality to be interpreted, always covered over by its forms of actualization; [that is to say] a theme or 'problematic' always covered over by its cases of solution. [*Difference and Repetition*, p. 186, emphasis added]

The economic instance, in other words, is a Problematic virtual structure (how to produce means of life to assure survival) to which various societies (or a given society at various times) propose differing actual Solutions—in much the same way that bird wings, fish fins, and mammalian legs provide differing actual Solutions to the biological Problem of locomotion in their struggles to survive [see *Difference and Repetition*, p. 207].

Given this understanding of modes of production as different ways human society self-organizes to address to the Problem of survival, Deleuze & Guattari go on to delineate (in *Anti-Oedipus*) three actual historical mechanisms of self-organization, which they call "coding" in the "savage" mode of production, "over-coding" in the "barbarian" mode of production, and "axiomatization" in the "civilized" or capitalist mode of production. Significantly, these Solutions all revolve around the management of **debt**; whereas Marx considered production to be primary, Deleuze & Guattari draw here on Nietzsche more than Marx, and instead consider debt to be the primary organizing element in any social formation. So how does society manage the Problems posed by economics? By organizing systems of debt relations that drive production and exchange: a patchwork of finite and temporary debts in the case of savagery; an infinite and one-way debt owed to the despot, head priest or king in barbarism; an equally infinite debt owed to capital in capitalism. These Solutions may be false (illusory, or "ideological"), but they are nonetheless effective in organizing production and exchange relations to address the Problem of survival in a distinctly human way.

In all three mega-strata, then, matter self-organizes in response to a variety of Problems, yet their means of self-organization differ Significantly. In the inorganic stratum, the self-organization of matter takes place on the same plane as matter itself; it is slow, and entails relatively few degrees of freedom. In the organic stratum, by contrast, the process of self-organization gets displaced onto a different plane, in the form of the genetic code; here, because of this displacement, the number of variations and the speed of variation accelerate dramatically. In the alloplastic stratum, finally, human self-organization takes place predominantly on the plane of Symbolic representation, using sounds, objects, and images to establish systems of debt and production—and the range of possibilities and speed of variation increase exponentially.

Concepts and problems

We are now in a position to survey the three principal types of categories Deleuze & Guattari use to analyze human Solutions to the ISSO Problem: typological, synthetic, and analytic. I have just outlined some of their broad typological categories, the most important of which are the State-form vs. the war-machine. But also important are the synthetic categories or "modes of libidinal production" originally outlined in the third chapter of *Anti-Oedipus*, but re-appearing here in *A Thousand Plateaus* in slightly different form—each of the three modes being itself a kind of Solution to the human ISSO Problem, as we have just seen. When we get to *A Thousand Plateaus*, the modern Solution is further analyzed in terms of an additional set of synthetic categories representing sub-Solutions: liberalism, fascism, totalitarianism and authoritarianism. But what is most distinctive methodologically about the later volume is the turn away from general, synthetic categories toward far more specific, analytic categories that distinguish at a finer degree of resolution the various components that compose the plane of the Symbolic Order on which the alloplastic stratum self-organizes. A libidinal mode of production will henceforth be understood as an assemblage of many different components, rather than a unity in its own right. Among the most important components of the Symbolic Order are language (along with regimes of signs) and money (as apparatus of capture). What is perhaps most important about these two vectors of social organization within the Symbolic Order, money and language, is how they interact with, and in some respects counter-act, each other, in important ways: they are vectors both of stratification and of de-stratification.

As a vehicle for the communication or imposition of common sense, language represents herd behavior, consolidates a stratum of shared orthodoxy, and shows strong affinities with territorialization and the State-form. In this context, money as medium for the cash nexus of the market fosters de-territorialization by de-coding the fixed meanings communicated by and as common sense. Yet as a vehicle for creative thought, language can articulate a variety of different versions of the ISSO Problem, and can also experiment with a whole range of potential Solutions. In fact, within the milieu of relative de-territorialization constituted by the world market, this is precisely the role of political philosophy as vector of absolute de-territorialization, as Deleuze & Guattari practice it in *A Thousand Plateaus* and later define it in *What is Philosophy?*. Concepts created by political philosophy (such as the ones I have just outlined) constitute so many different ways of articulating the human ISSO Problem, often in relation to non-human or pre-Symbolic versions of the ISSO Problem (as we have seen), and sometimes (but not necessarily) in the form of potential Solutions to that Problem. Like their precursors the wolves, political philosophers play around with different social roles (or conceptual personae), with different virtual types of sociality (herds/packs/flocks), and with different actual modes of social organization (savage/despotic/civilized)—and the point of thought-experimenting in these ways is to map the vast virtual potential for self-organization of the human life-form as it emerges from the processes of chaosmosis, from the evolution of life on planet earth, and from the history of our species. As thought-experiments, the conceptual personae of political philosophy—such as the schizo-revolutionary, the minor, the nomad—are derived from and created in relation to a given socio-historical milieu in order to map its strata according to their lines of de-stratification, and in order therefore to be able to feed back into that socio-historical milieu some practical experiments aimed at realizing its virtual potential to self-organize differently, and to become better than it is.

So the Problems posed in the fifteen plateaus of *A Thousand Plateaus* ultimately break down into five kinds:

- **epistemological**: how can thought operate in such a way that it thinks with the cosmos instead of about it, and is therefore able to accelerate the relative de-territorialization of the milieus it is sometimes fortunate to inhabit to the point of reaching the infinite speed of absolute de-territorialization, or pure immanence? The plateaus on the "Rhizome" and "The Smooth and the Striated" address this Problem most directly, along with the portions of the Nomadology plateau dealing with royal and nomad science and the differences between axiomatics and problematics. The point here is to develop an image of thought best suited to mapping being in terms of becoming, and the actual in terms of the virtual.

- **ontological**: how can the cosmos and Life within it exist in such a way that they are the result of constant change yet are also always susceptible to further change? How can we understand being in terms of becoming, in terms of difference rather than identity, as a function of the dynamics of open systems? And most importantly, what is the payoff of understanding the world this way? How does it improve our prospects for social change? It is the Geology of Morals plateau along with the Refrain plateau that address this Problem most directly and comprehensively—the first mostly for the inorganic stratum, and the second mostly for the alloplastic stratum.

- **anthropological**—a third kind of Problem could be called anthropological, but only in the structuralist (and anti-humanist) sense involving the Symbolic Order: how does the human life-form occupy the alloplastic stratum Symbolically; how is human social self-organization accomplished through and reflected in signs—through language, money, and images? Here the plateaus on the Postulates of Linguistics, Regimes of Signs, Faciality and the Apparatus of Capture are the relevant ones.

- **ethical**: how can human individuals self-organize so as to maximize their chances for productive and enjoyable de-stratification with others? "How Do You Make Yourself a Body without Organs?" is the plateau of most obvious relevance here; but "One or Several Wolves," "Three Novellas," and the Becomings plateau also address ethical Problems.

- **political**: how can the human life-form be understood to self-organize socially in a way that accounts for herd as well as pack behaviors, for repressive despotic tyranny as well as expansive economic imperialism, for the constraints of rigid stratification as well as flights of de-stratification? Along with the plateau on Nomadology, the Micropolitics and Segmentarity plateau addresses this Problem most directly, although many other plateaus do so in less obvious ways.

The next chapter examines how the book treats each of these five Problems, starting with epistemology.

CHAPTER THREE

Reading the Text

EPISTEMOLOGY

The Problem: How can thought operate in such a way that it thinks **with** the cosmos instead of **about** it, and is therefore able to accelerate the relative de-territorialization of the milieus it is sometimes fortunate to inhabit to the point of reaching the infinite speed of absolute de-territorialization, or pure immanence? What image of thought is best suited to mapping being in terms of becoming, and the actual in terms of the virtual?

The Primary Sources: the Rhizome plateau, The Smooth and the Striated plateau, and Propositions III and IV of the Nomadology plateau (on royal and nomad science and noology).

The overview just presented in the previous chapter may have seemed like a story—starting with the Big Bang, crossing a number of significant thresholds: the emergence of stars, of Life, of social species, and so on—and ending with political philosophy as experimentation with the Problem of Intra-Species Social Organization. But those thresholds are not really arrayed in a linear order: they are thresholds among basins of attraction that co-exist, rather than stages that supersede one another as if part of some vast cosmic history. Partly in order to dispel any impression of linear historicity (an impression unfortunately suggested by the discursive form of *Anti-Oedipus*, if not its content), *A Thousand Plateaus* is arranged by dated plateaus—and not only do those dates not line up in chronological order, they don't even belong to a common temporal scale (e.g. 10,000 BC and November 28, 1947). Each plateau—and there must be somewhere between 15 and 1,000 of them—stages a thought-experiment on the creation or renewal of a concept or assemblage of concepts. Now philosophical concepts are not Platonic Ideas: they are always extracted from actual states of affairs outside of philosophy, from a pre-conceptual Event that contributes to the virtual domain something that some philosopher deems to be of lasting significance. In this respect, philosophers themselves can be considered Events (or their philosophies can be), and so can the discoveries of other disciplines—science, art, ethnography, mathematics, literature, and so on—so that the creation of concepts extracted from actual states of affairs is accompanied by the creation of philosophical concepts out of the fruits of other disciplines, as well as by the renewal of concepts from previous philosophies. In any case, a plateau's date marks the moment or circumstance when a given pre-conceptual Event achieved its maximum actual historical intensity so far, even though its lasting significance is by definition not limited to that moment, and even though it may repeat with less intensity in circumstances before or after the dated Event. The aim of philosophy in extracting concepts from outside Events is to take them to the limit of thought (absolute de-territorialization at infinite speed), to maximize their intensity, to develop their transformative or catalytic potential to the utmost for eventual re-insertion into other circumstances in order to change them—hopefully for the better. (This is true for critical as well as affirmative concepts: the aim is to maximize the diagnostic force of the concept of "faciality" as well as the constructive force of "nomad science," for example.)

Philosophy thus always operates "in-between"—or better: *au milieu*, which here means both in context, in situation (as Sartre might say; not universally) and in-between the pre-philosophical states of affairs and disciplines from which it extracts philosophical potential (to become-otherwise, to become-better) and post-philosophical activities (i.e. experimentation) in the world, where that potential gets proven or disproven—at least for the time being. What the philosophical concept extracts from outside circumstances or disciplines, that is to say, is not an essence or a position but a tendency, an orientation-to-change. "Nowhere do we claim for our concepts the title of science," Deleuze & Guattari insist [22].

In other words, the question of philosophy is never "What is it?" (the question of being), but "In which direction is it going?" "How fast?" "Along with what else?" Ultimately, the core philosophical question is not "What **is** it?" but "What can **become** of it?" And what specific tendency or becoming a given philosophy detects in and extracts from the outside depends crucially on the **image of thought** by which that philosophy operates. Every philosophy has a specific orientation that distinguishes it from other philosophies, by selecting the Problem(s) it will address, constructing its manner of addressing them, and determining what kind(s) of Solution(s) to propose, if any. And that image of thought will select what tendency or tendencies its concepts extract from the outside under consideration. Of course, this presupposes a minimum threshold of correct understanding of states of affairs and of other disciplines on philosophy's part: the outside tendency must in some sense really correlate or connect with the philosophical orientation—so that a double-becoming can take place between them. But tendency-selection nonetheless remains more of an art than a science—one has to have a nose for it, as Nietzsche might say.

It must be said, however, that the image of thought has an ambiguous status in *A Thousand Plateaus*—and this very ambiguity can serve here as a frame for the question of epistemology. As I will show, this question tends to revolve around the differences between striated space and smooth space, between royal science and minor science, and between the State-form of thought and nomad thought. But the ambiguity arises because nomad thought taken to its limit—which is, after all, the aim of philosophy—would end up without any image of thought whatsoever. The speed and orientation of thought would correlate with the speed and orientation of the outside so precisely that the image of thought between them would become unnecessary and disappear entirely: thought would become completely immanent to the situation. The nomadic "form of exteriority of thought," Deleuze & Guattari explain, is ultimately "not... *another image* in opposition to the image inspired by the State apparatus. It is rather a force that destroys both the image *and* its copies, the model *and* its reproductions..." [377]. And yet the book opens with precisely an image of thought: the rhizome; and it comes full circle with a plateau devoted entirely to models (of smooth and striated space) at the end![1] They admit to having written the book "as a rhizome...

composed of plateaus," and claim to "have given it a circular form... only for laughs" [22], but I'm convinced there is more to it than that. For in a sense they **had** to give their book a circular form, opening with a plateau devoted to images of thought (the tree as well as the rhizome) and closing with models of space (smooth and striated)—for what would it look like if high-speed, image-free nomad thought were finally to arrive in the final plateau? It would look like a traditional, tree-form book with a linear argument and a rousing conclusion. The characterization of plateaus they derive from Gregory Bateson—"continuous, self-vibrating region[s] of intensities whose development avoids any orientation toward a culmination point or external end" [22]—surely applies equally to the book as a whole. So aptly enough, their thought reaches its highest speeds not at the end, but *au milieu*: in the middle—and going in all directions. "The middle (*le milieu*) is by no means an average," they say; "on the contrary it is where things pick up speed" [25]. So if they begin with two opposed images of thought, rhizome and tree, they are in effect "invok[ing] one dualism only in order to challenge another"—in this case, the book as representation of the world, among others:

> We employ a dualism of models only in order to arrive at a process that challenges all models. Each time, mental correctives are necessary to undo the dualisms we had no wish to construct but through which we pass. Arrive at the magic formula we all seek—PLURALISM = MONISM—via all the dualisms that are the enemy, an entirely necessary enemy, the furniture we are forever rearranging. [20–1]

And if they end with an indefinite number of models (they are "well aware that there are many others," they insist [499]), it is in order to instantiate the "logic of the AND"—for while "the tree imposes the verb 'to be,' ... the fabric of the rhizome is the conjunction, 'and... and... and...' " [25]. (The "logic of the AND" corresponds to what in *Anti-Oedipus* Deleuze & Guattari called the "connective synthesis of production.")

"Introduction: rhizome"

So what does the rhizome offer us as an image of thought, and as a format for writing a book? For one thing, it enables us to think **with** the world, rather than thinking about the world—in both senses of the term "with": we think with the world in the sense of using the world as a tool to think with, and in the sense of thinking along with the world the way it itself thinks. (Early-modern Dutch philosopher Baruch Spinoza is the probably the most important of Deleuze's precursors to insist that thought is an objective attribute of the world, not just of thinking subjects.) Extracting concepts from Events in the outside world is a way of thinking with the world. Thinking about the world, by contrast, introduces the apparatus of representation-signification between us and the world—something Deleuze & Guattari are keen to avoid. Representation and signification belong to and perpetuate the tree image of thought, imposing a one-to-one (or "bi-univocal") relation of signification between two terms—whether signifier and signified or sign and referent. Deleuze & Guattari prefer the perspective of Danish linguist Louis Hjelmslev, for whom two planes, the expression-plane and the content-plane, co-exist in what he called "reciprocal presupposition" with one another. Reciprocal presupposition means that neither term has priority or precedence over the other; they are mutually constitutive of one another. Written as a rhizome, then, the book does not represent or reproduce the world (as its referent), nor signify the meaning of the world (as its signified), but connects and articulates itself in reciprocal presupposition with the world. Somewhat like Saussure's planes of signifier and signified, which are structures of pure relations, both discourse and the outside world for Deleuze & Guattari are "heterogeneous multiplicities," that is, each is composed of innumerable elements co-existing in the simplest, zero-degree mode of relation possible, as designated by the logic of "and... and... and..." (this and that and this and...). The challenge for a rhizome-book is to "find an adequate outside with which to assemble in heterogeneity, rather than a world to reproduce" [24]. And the aim of the book-outside articulation or assemblage is not to represent the world as it is or what it means, but to survey and map its tendencies or becomings, for better and for worse.

Deleuze & Guattari contrast the rhizome-book they are writing with two other book-forms and corresponding modes or images of arborescent thought, which they characterize as the tap-root book and the fascicular-root book. The tap-root book is organized around a single principle of coherence or meaning (often the intention, genius, or authority of the author) in order to represent the world or a privileged perspective on it. This type of book is both self-contained, in that it is perfectly coherent internally, and yet also relates to the external world, by reflecting or representing it. Fascicular roots are multiple rather than single, but fascicular-root books retain key properties of the tap-root book. As confidence in the tap-root book's ability to completely comprehend and faithfully represent the external world wanes, that very inability becomes the principle of the fascicular-book's coherence, even as the ultimate meaning of such a book gets infinitely deferred and/or requires endless interpretation. "The world has become chaos," Deleuze & Guattari conclude, "but the book remains the image of the world: radicle [fascicular] chaosmos rather than root-cosmos [resulting in] a strange mystification: a book all the more total for being fragmented" [6]. As we will see, these arborescent images of thought bear a certain resemblance to forms of the Despotic Face (the radiant or full-frontal face and the averted face), as well as to forms of physics (deterministic and probabilistic). But the main function of outlining these two tree-forms of the book is to better present the rhizomatic book-form, which has several distinctive features.

The first feature is connectability: any rhizomatic element has the potential to connect with any other element. Take felt as an instance of a rhizome, contrasted with fabric. Two strands belonging to either the warp or the woof of a piece of fabric will never intersect; but any two strands of fiber in felt, depending on their length, may intersect with any other, and the connections among them are multiple and random. In fact, the strength of felt arises precisely from the number and omni-directionality of the intersections. The disadvantage of felt as an illustration, however (and this is true of botanical illustrations as well), is that its components (fibers) are homogeneous, whereas philosophically speaking, the rhizome is essentially heterogeneous, its second key feature. In the philosophical sense, "a rhizome ceaselessly establishes connections [among] semiotic chains, organizations of power, and circumstances relative to the arts, sciences, and social struggles" [7]. Even on its own plane, discourse as rhizome is "an essentially heterogeneous reality" [7]—a "throng of dialects, patois, slangs, and specialized languages," Deleuze & Guattari assert, with "no mother tongue" [7]. The appearance of a standard language is instead the result of a power-takeover by one language among many, necessarily in connection with yet other factors, most notably political and demographic ones.

A third feature of philosophical rhizomes is multiplicity. Rhizomatic elements co-exist with one another, but without structure (e.g. felt). Any structure or unity is imposed as an extra dimension, as we saw with Proust, and as an effect of power on the dimensions of co-existence of the rhizome itself, whose **self-organization** requires no added dimensions: structuration or unification, by contrast, occurs as the result of "over-coding" by a signifier (e.g., the phallus, the name of the Father, the Word of God or Despot) and/or a corresponding process of subjectification (involving e.g., a castrated subject, an obedient child, a faithful believer or subject). There are no pre-determined positions or points within a rhizomatic multiplicity, only lines along with random nodes arising at the haphazard intersections of them (felt). Moreover, because they are heterogeneous multiplicities, philosophical rhizomes develop like a crazy patchwork quilt in unforeseen directions (unlike fabric, which can only get longer, not wider) and in unforeseen ways; this is a fourth feature. Indeed, rhizomes are philosophically defined at the limit by their outside, by the "lines of flight" that connect them outside of themselves and transform them. Thus to take one of Deleuze and Guattari's favorite examples, the orchid and the wasp each de-territorializes the surface-coloring code of the other, only to re-territorialize it for their own sake, as part of the reproductive system of the orchid, and of the nutritional motor-schema of the wasp. This is another instance of double-becoming, which is known in biology as "a-parallel evolution." Along this line, but also because of the discovery of the widespread transfer of genetic information across evolutionary lines, biology has had to abandon the old tree-model of evolutionary descent in favor of a rhizomatic model, where "transversal communications [among] different lines scramble the genealogical trees" [11]. "The same applies to the book," Deleuze & Guattari want to suggest: the rhizome-book is "not an image of the world... it forms a rhizome with the world [so that] there is an a-parallel evolution of the book and the world" [11], a double-becoming of book and world. (At least that's the hope, "if [the book] is capable" [11]: it's no doubt quicker and easier to de-territorialize in writing than in the world—speed as simultaneously the boon and bane of philosophical thought.)

In order to pursue double-becomings with the world, or to think **with** it, as I have said, a rhizome-book must be cartographic rather than photographic—and this is a fifth feature of the rhizome: mapping is distinct from—and preferable to—tracing. Tracing merely reproduces its object fixed in representation; mapping indicates its tendencies and potential for change. "What distinguishes the map from the tracing," Deleuze & Guattari explain, "is that [the map] is entirely oriented toward an experimentation in contact with the real" [12]. And they are expressly critical of genetic and structural models of tracing, which predominate in psychoanalysis and linguistics. What such models do is stabilize and neutralize the inexhaustible mobility of the multiplicity they are tracing according to the predetermined axes and coordinates inherent in the model, so that instead of reproducing the object in all its indeterminacy and mobility, the tracing simply reproduces the model itself. (This is a procedure Deleuze & Guattari target throughout the psychoanalytic literature, from Freud to Klein to Lacan.)

> That is why the tracing is so dangerous. It injects redundancies and propagates them. What the tracing reproduces of the map or rhizome are only the impasses, blockages, incipient taproots, or points of structuration. Take a look at psychoanalysis and linguistics: all the former has ever made are tracings or photos of the unconscious, and the latter of language, with all the betrayals that implies (it's not surprising that psychoanalysis tied its fate to that of linguistics). [13]

Mapping, by contrast, follows various lines of a multiplicity, evaluates and experiments with their escape-velocities, evaluates their potential for transformation, and highlights or intensifies the lines of flight. Of what significance to philosophy would a wasp be, if not for its line-of-flight and its double-becoming with the orchid? (Philosophy is thinking **with** the world again here.)

Then again, it is also true in another sense that philosophy thinks with the brain. But the brain itself is a rhizome, with its neurons, axons, and dendrites forming a dense meshwork of meta-stable connections rather than a stable, centered tree-structure. Along the same line, computer and information sciences have recently taken interest in neural networking as an alternative to command-tree hierarchies, developing in place of linear, centered systems a kind of a-centered system consisting of

> finite networks of automata in which communication runs from any neighbor to any other, the stems or channels do not preexist, and all individuals are interchangeable, defined only by their *state* at a given moment—such that the local operations are coordinated and the final, global result synchronized without a central agency. [17]

This Solution to the Problem of coordinated action is not peculiar to computer science, however—or to humans, for that matter: for this is precisely the way birds flock and fish school, as multiplicities and through the strictly local communication of intensive states of speed and direction among members of the flock or school. (There we go, thinking with the world again.) This is not to say that the human brain always works in this fashion; in fact long-term memory appears to be more or less arborescent and centralized. But short-term memory is thoroughly rhizomatic, and so Deleuze & Guattari advocate writing a book using short-term memory and what they call "short-term ideas" [17]—perhaps one reason (among many, no doubt) that their categories are in constant flux, and vary from plateau to plateau. That is certainly the reason they end the Rhizome plateau with a call to write with slogans: "Make rhizomes, not roots, never plant! Don't sow, grow offshoots!... Run lines, never plot a point!... Have short-term ideas. Make maps, not photos..." [24–5].

"The Smooth and the Striated"

The Smooth and Striated plateau begins with an acknowledgement of just such a slippage of categories from one plateau to another, and then goes on to show how the smooth/striated opposition varies across a series of six different models of space. So, having started by simply aligning the distinction between smooth and striated space with the distinctions between nomad and sedentary space and between war-machine and State space, Deleuze & Guattari insist on "a much more complex difference by virtue of which the successive terms of the oppositions fail to coincide entirely" [474]. Moreover, although they maintain that the *de jure* distinction between the two types of space is significant, they insist at the same time that the two exist *de facto* only in mixtures and in passages from one to the other (and there is even a third, hybrid form of space they call "holey space"). In this respect, it would be better to use verb forms designating movements or processes than substantives or adjectives denoting fixed types: smoothing is a process that can happen to striated space, just as striation is an operation that can befall smooth space. Smoothing and striating are more evocative names for processes that function as abstract machines operating on widely different materials, as the subsequent survey of models clearly shows. It is not necessary to examine all six models in detail; and anyway, this summary plateau near the end of the book is not where its most interesting thinking is likely to take place, as I have suggested. But I will try to indicate briefly why, out of the indefinite number of possible models, these six were selected for review, despite the drastic over-simplification this will entail.

> *The Musical Model* Contemporary French composer Pierre Boulez coined the terms in the first place, asserting that one occupies a smooth space without counting, and counts in order to occupy a striated space. His use of the terms also makes it clear that in both forms of space, issues of temporality—including frequency, interval, and rhythm—are also crucial. Smooth and striated are thus better understood as types of "space-time." They overlap significantly with the key terms *nomos* and *logos* from the Nomadology plateau, while the entire discussion resonates substantially with the Refrain plateau and the final "becoming-music" section of the Becomings plateau. Perhaps most important: rhizomes constitute and operate in smooth space, and nomads occupy space without counting.
>
> *The Technological Model* This is the first model to be presented in the series, perhaps because the leading

examples of felt and fabric are so familiar and clear (although the subsequent distinction between patchwork and embroidery may be less so). But there is also a connection made between striation and the State-form of thought starting with Plato, who used weaving to illustrate State rule.

The Maritime Model Submarine warfare is offered as a quintessential example of a war-machine operating in smooth space, but long before the invention of submarines, the oceans represented the purest challenge to striation, since maritime space is already homogeneous (usually a key result of striation) and has no landmarks or "singularities" to obviate the need for positioning via latitude and longitude. In contrast with the sea, the city is considered the most striated space, reinforcing the strong affinities between *polis* and *logos*.

The Physical Model The ancient Greeks (from Democritus to Lucretius) developed a science of smooth space, which was then largely forgotten or suppressed in the development of Enlightenment mechanistic science. Striated space subsequently became central to the notion of "work" deployed in both modern physics and modern political economy, following from the distinction between the "free action" taking place in the smooth space-time of a-cephalous (State-less) societies and "work," which takes place in the striated space-times of both imperial-despotic and capitalist social formations. This leads in turn to the distinction between striated and smooth capital, the former epitomized by Taylorization in the factory and the latter by the instantaneous circulation of finance capital across the globe and the attendant impossibility of pinpointing the locus of surplus-value.[2]

The Aesthetic Model – subtitled *Nomad Art* The smooth/striated distinction does not align with the distinction between local and global. Instead Deleuze & Guattari propose the distinction between the local absolute and the relative global. In the smooth space of the nomad, the local is absolute because where you are is the only point of reference, and heterogeneous space unfolds strictly in terms of what direction you are going and at what speed. Striated space is relative and global because any given position is relative to all others as they are plotted in a homogeneous metric space that encompasses (and over-codes) the entire globe.

The Mathematical Model This section picks up on the earlier discussion of smooth space as a "patchwork" (the opening image of the plateau is a patchwork quilt), and connects it to the rigors of Reimannian mathematics and non-Euclidean geometry.[3] Roughly parallel distinctions between two kinds of geometry—major and minor— and between two kinds of number—nomadic numbers and State-centric numbers; "numbering numbers" and "numbered numbers"—reinforce the distinction already proposed in the Nomadology plateau between royal and nomad science—to which I will turn next.

But first let us note the irony of the command they issue immediately after surveying these six models of space: "Do not multiply models" [499]. For one thing, this statement reinforces the book's larger irony of opening with images of thought and closing with models of space, when its main thrust is to get beyond models and images of thought altogether. The plateau then concludes with a different kind of admonition: "Never believe that a smooth space will suffice to save us" [500]. This is particularly important in light of their account of contemporary global capital's tendency to generate and occupy smooth space. The distinction of smooth space remains critical, however, for even if "smooth spaces are not in themselves liberatory, ... the struggle is changed or displaced in them, and life reconstitutes its stakes, confronts new obstacles, switches adversaries" [500]. Smooth capital represents just such a new adversary, and the clear implication is that struggles against it must reconstitute their modes of resistance accordingly.

"Treatise on Nomadology—the War-Machine" (1)

Propositions III and IV of the Nomadology plateau expand on the distinction between the State form of thought and nomad thought, declaring that "the exteriority of the war machine [vis-à-vis the State] is... attested to by epistemology, which intimates the existence and perpetuation of a 'nomad' or 'minor' science.... [and] is attested to, finally, by noology" [361, 374]. (By "noology," Deleuze & Guattari mean the study of images of thought.) Here is where the State-form of thought receives its most complete diagnosis. State thought is stratified thought. Its basis is the double-articulation of State power and universal reason, each of which enables and augments the other: the power of the State provides reason with a reality and a proper space of its own, an "interiority," as Deleuze & Guattari call it; and the universality of reason grants the State its universal justification. "Only thought is capable of inventing the fiction of a State that is universal by right," they insist, "[only thought is capable] of elevating the State to the level of *de jure* universality" [375]. At the same time, each of these articulated planes is itself a double-articulation: State power, as delineated in the opening pages of the plateau, is founded on the double-articulation of the Despot and the legislator, the binder and the organizer; universal reason, in turn, is composed of the double-articulation of an empire of Truth and a republic of free minds.[4] It is Plato, of course, who represents the advent or inaugural "Event" of State thought (one reason the Problem of over-turning Platonism is central to Deleuze's work). In Plato's *Republic* of "free minds," the despotic "Philosopher-King" has command of the Truth, and citizens are "free" to be who they "really" are to the precise extent that they accede to the universality of reason and disown their unhealthy appetites and inordinate ambitions. Here, the two poles of the articulation seem rather far apart and out of balance in favor of the Despot, to our modern eyes anyway—probably because Kant has long since merged them for us. For with Kant, legislator and citizen, imperious Truth and assenting minds, both converge under the imperative: "Be reasonable: obey yourself." This modern refrain finds echoes in famous German idealist G. W. F. Hegel's philosophy of State reason, of course, but also in the Republican sociology of French sociologist Emile Durkheim, among others.

Nomad thought

This situation—the apparent ubiquity of State thought—gives rise to the second formal Problem posed by the Nomadology plateau. The first Problem was *"Is there a way of warding off the formation of a State apparatus?"* [356], and the second, *"Is there a way to extricate thought from the State model?"* [374]. To which the answer is yes: the way out is comprised of what Deleuze & Guattari call the "outside thought" of the nomad war-machine [376], as expressed in a host of iconoclastic thinkers such as Søren Kierkegaarde, Friedrich Nietzsche, Antonin Artaud, Heinrich von Kleist, Maurice Blanchot, and others.[5] At the limit, nomad thought becomes practically impossible to define, because it has no image of thought of its own: it destroys all images of thought and eliminates "every possibility of subordinating thought to a model of the True, the Just, or the Right" [377]. These models, along with the State-form of thought in general, are based on method, which stipulates the path that thought must follow through striated space from one point to the next in its procedure (e.g. first doubt, then conceive clearly, then guarantee results [as per René Descartes' *Discourse on Method*]). Nomad thought, however, has no method: at each point in its proceeding, it must select a direction on the spot, depending on a punctual evaluation of the outside forces in play at a given juncture. "In the smooth space of Zen," Deleuze & Guattari suggest (mischievously scrambling the code of philosophy with an image of thought from outside its proper boundaries), "the arrow does not go from one point to another but is taken up at any point, to be sent to any other point, and tends to permute with the archer and the target" [377]. Imagine the trajectory of an arrow in flight, fixed by neither the archer who shot it nor the target at which it was aimed—just try! Is this an image of thought? But isn't this precisely what it means for thought to take flight "au milieu" (in the middle)? And isn't this precisely how birds flock, and how jazz musicians improvise? (Does thinking **with** the world like this comprise an image of thought, or obviate the need for one?)

Yet even if nomad thought cannot be methodologically defined, surely some of its proceedings can be rendered visible, or at least hinted at suggestively. So Deleuze & Guattari contrast the maxim, which belongs to State-thought, with the nomad aphorism (and its great practitioner, Nietzsche): the maxim as closed form commands obedience, whereas an aphorism as open form incites interpretation, and "always awaits its meaning from a new external force… that must conquer or subjugate it [in order to] utilize it" [377]. Nomad thought is tactical rather than strategic (in the sense French poststructuralist philosopher Michel de Certeau derives from Prussian military theorist von Clausewitz): it moves at variable speed and direction through a vectorial space rather than constructing stable universal models in striated space. It is as if at any point in its trajectory, the arrow were to make instantaneous and short-term adjustments to compensate for cross-wind velocities, the initial aims of the archer long forgotten, and the target itself constantly shifting position and direction—the target of smooth capital, for instance, as a new adversary and moving target. **It is the frequency and degree of such adjustments that determine what Deleuze & Guattari mean by the "speed" of thought (the arrow), not its velocity toward a target.** In contrast with slow-speed methods, which stipulate velocity and direction in advance, high-speed nomad thought is distinguished by its ability to encompass or survey all the Significant contingencies of the Event or Problematic situation it is mapping: indeed, it is because nomad thought moves at **infinite** speed that it **can** map **all** the Significant contingencies that "belong to philosophy by right" (as Deleuze & Guattari put it in *What is Philosophy?*), without being slowed or (mis-)directed by a pre-existing method or image of thought. It is thereby able to always keep even a moving target in sight.

Nomad thought thus matches an account of thought Deleuze shared with French poststructuralist philosopher and intellectual historian Michel Foucault: it intervenes as a kind of relay "in-between" an older practical orientation to the world which has exhausted its power to incite change and another, newer and hopefully more productive one. Here is Deleuze & Guattari's portrait of nomad thought: it is thought

> grappling with exterior forces instead of being gathered up in an interior form, operating by relays instead of forming an image; [it is] an event-thought... instead of a subject-thought, a problem-thought instead of an essence-thought or theorem; a thought that appeals to a people instead of taking itself for a government ministry. [378]

And the nature of this appeal is crucial. It is not an appeal to a people constituted as citizen-Subjects of the Republic of Reason in striated space, where Truth encompasses the Whole of Being, and Being then gets converted by the rational Subject into being-for-us.

Rather, the appeal takes place in a vectorial space of Problems, operates by contagion or by inspiring enthusiasm, and is addressed to a people-to-come, as Deleuze & Guattari repeatedly put it, who themselves must issue from an oppressed race or tribe. Drawing on French avant-garde poet Arthur Rimbaud (as they have since *Anti-Oedipus*), they insist that nomad thought "does not ally itself with a universal thinking subject but, on the contrary, with a singular race" [379], and its double-articulation does not link a Universal Subject of Reason to the Truth of the Whole, but rather takes place between an oppressed race or group operating as a pack or tribe and a Problematic smooth space or absolute-local "milieu," in a reciprocal double-becoming of them both.

Nomad science

How does "problem-thought" differ from "essence-thought" or theorematic thought? This is one of the issues that Proposition III of the Nomadology plateau addresses, by distinguishing nomad or minor science from royal or State science. Although State science has predominated in the West, especially since the Enlightenment, nomad science has a long, largely subterranean history stretching back to ancient Greece, and it continues to play a role today, even under the dominion of State science. Modern State science has operated according to two basic forms or images of thought over the past several centuries. The first form was Newtonian mechanics, according to which time was reversible and the universe was completely predictable and deterministic. The second form was thermodynamics, according to which time was irreversible (as expressed in the famous second law of thermodynamics, the law of entropy) and the universe was no longer completely predictable but only probabilistic. So, given a finite amount of energy (which can neither be created not destroyed, according to the first law of thermodynamics), the universe would inevitably and irreversibly tend (according to the law of entropy) toward its most probable state (sometimes referred to as "heat death"): the absolutely even distribution of matter and energy throughout the universe, and the cancellation of all differences. Newtonian mechanics made the universe deterministically predictable by restricting the number of variables that could vary in a given calculation; linear thermodynamics made it probabilistically predictable by assuming that the universe was a closed system. The non-linear complexity science on which Deleuze & Guattari draw, however, accepts the irreversibility of time, but treats the universe as an open system (a "chaosmos"), thereby allowing for processes of emergence and self-organization. And the orientation to Problems characteristic of nomad science makes it particularly adept at following such processes, as we shall see.

Deleuze & Guattari begin their discussion of nomad science by outlining four of its key features:

1) It foregrounds fluids rather than solids, and thus

2) emphasizes becoming and heterogeneity rather than the stability and constancy characteristic of solid-state physics.

3) Its basic figures are the unpredictable swerve (Lucretius' *clinamen*) and the vortex rather than the straight line and the polygon, and its background consists of open, Reimannian, smooth space (also characterized as vectorial or topological space) rather than the closed, Euclidean, striated space typified by the Cartesian coordinate system.

4) "Finally," they say, nomad science is "problematic rather than theorematic"—which I would say as a first approximation likens it to "bricolage" as defined by French anthropologist Claude Lévi-Strauss in contrast with engineering: nomad science operates by «rule of thumb,» with whatever resources happen to be at hand, rather than by strict adherence to the supposed "laws" of nature or physics promulgated by State science, and by acquiring and/or producing everything that is needed according to a pre-ordained plan.

As an illustration, they describe two different techniques used to build cathedrals in pre-Enlightenment Europe. One technique involved building from a pre-drawn plan of the complete edifice, from which templates were derived in order to govern the quarrying and finish-cutting of the building-stones long before they were put in place. The other technique involved building on the spot, so to speak, literally from the ground up, with journeymen cutting stones to fit by rule of thumb as they proceeded, and compensating as they went along for the peculiar shape of one stone by fitting the next one to it, and so on. In this connection, it makes sense that the concepts of State science would be clear and distinct, whereas those of nomad science appear vague: the circle is an idea (and an ideal) belonging to State science; "roundness" is a concrete, perceptible—yet always imprecise—property typical of nomad science. "The State is perpetually producing and reproducing ideal circles," Deleuze & Guattari maintain, "but a [nomad] war-machine is necessary to make something round" [367]. More important than the *de jure* distinction between building techniques, however, is that they express two very different modes of work and modes of life—here embodied in the group of journeymen stone-cutters on one hand, and church architects and project overseers on the other—which are in perpetual struggle with one another. There are in effect "two formally different conceptions of science," Deleuze & Guattari explain, competing over what is "ontologically a single field of interaction in which royal science continually appropriates the contents of ... nomad science while nomad science continually cuts the contents of royal science loose" [367]. Then suddenly, in the midst of what appeared to be an epistemological discussion of the sciences, the Problem of "What is a collective *body*?" [366] crops up!

In an important sense, this is the central topic of the Nomadology plateau as a whole, as we will see in subsequent sections: nomadism expresses a specific type of social cohesion, one kind of Solution to the human Intra-Species Social Organization Problem, and the State-form comprises another. Of crucial relevance here is the claim that "nomad science does not have the same relation to work as [State] science" [368]. In fact, the State was (and is) constantly at odds with groups such as journeymen stonecutters, whose mobility and autonomy were a threat to its command and control. The State Solution was (and is) to devise and enforce a strict division between intellectual and manual labor, by insisting (in this case) that cathedrals be built according to pre-designed plan, and by reducing stone-cutting to the mere execution of mechanical tasks at the command of the architects (and in this light, it appears as no accident that the Russian-American neoliberal novelist Ayn Rand would choose an architect for the hero of her most influential fable). Both forms of science involve the construction of planes, Deleuze & Guattari explain, but

> the ground-level plane of the Gothic journeyman is opposed to the metric plane of the architect, which is on paper and off

site. The [journeyman's] plane of consistency or composition is opposed to another plane, that of organization or formation. Stone cutting by squaring is opposed to stone cutting using templates, which implies the erection of a model for reproduction. [368]

As is already evident, however, this opposition is not merely an epistemological one: it is at the same time a social and political one, in reciprocal presupposition with one another. Significantly, the State's battle against nomad sciences arises "not because the content of these sciences is inexact or imperfect... but because they [entail] a division of labor opposed to the norms of the State" [368]. Central to State rule and the State form of thought, that is to say, is the abstract machine that Deleuze & Guattari (following French philosopher Gilbert Simondon) refer to as **hylomorphism**.

A mainstay of State philosophy since Aristotle, the doctrine of hylomorphism holds that matter is undifferentiated and devoid of qualities until it gets imbued with them by form; form imposes qualities on inert matter; matter must obey laws or remain a pure undifferentiated chaos. This is a view that recent complexity science has by now thoroughly debunked and rejected. The critique of hylomorphism entails a critical distinction between procedures of **following** and **reproducing**. State science is based on the principle of reproduction: not only does inert matter produce nothing on its own account, merely reproducing the properties and behaviors assigned to it by formal laws, but those laws only count as scientific if they can be reproduced with absolute certainty through repeated experiments. Any variations are discounted as mere accidents or weeded out through statistical regression analysis or other means. The nomadic principle of following is very different. As the ancient Greeks were among the earliest to realize, fluid dynamics (unlike solid dynamics in most cases) cannot be predicted or reproduced— they can only be followed. (For example, it is impossible to predict on which side of a flowing stream of liquid an eddy will form, as it inevitably will when the flow reaches a certain threshold velocity.) And precisely the same is true in evolutionary science: the trajectory of evolution cannot be predicted with any certainty: it can only be followed *ex post facto*. From Lucretius to Darwin to Heisenberg and beyond, following has been and remains an important principle of science, despite its incompatibility with hylomorphism. Yet the latter continues to inform much of what goes on in the social and human sciences, including in philosophy itself. One reason the State form of thought is so powerful is that hylomorphism applies so seamlessly to questions of epistemology, economics and politics alike. Homologous oppositions elevating intellectual over manual labor, rulers over the ruled, soul over body, and form over matter echo one another like refrains and reinforce the reign of State power and the authority of State thought simultaneously.

Nomad science distinguishes itself from State science in yet another way. The principle of verification by reproduction informing State science, as we have seen, requires that experimental results be reproduced independent of circumstances; within the parameters set by controlled variables, the same result will always occur, no matter when, where, or by whom the experiments are conducted. The theorematic power of State science is achieved by isolating its experimental operations from any particular conditions "on the ground" at a specific time, thereby making its results appear eternal and universal. (This perspective makes no sense for a nomad science such as evolutionary biology, since if you rewind and re-run evolution on earth 100 times, as I've said, there could be up to 100 different results.) Nomad science, by contrast, operates without the autonomy and theorematic certainty of State science, experimenting "en plein air," as Deleuze & Guattari so colorfully put it [374]—that is to say in concrete circumstances "on the ground" where the control of variables enabling the erection of stable theoretical models is impossible. In such circumstances, Deleuze & Guattari maintain, "nomad sciences quickly overstep the possibility of calculation: they inhabit that 'more' that exceeds the space of reproduction and soon run into problems that are insurmountable from that point of view; they eventually resolve those problems by means of a real-life operation" [374]. In contrast to the autonomy and claim to universality of State science, then, the orientation of nomad science is thoroughly pragmatic: it addresses Problems encountered in the outside world (not hypotheses assigned to it by its own theory, as in State science), and its results depend on a "whole set of collective, non-scientific activities" [374] that validate those results only to the (necessarily limited) extent that the Problematic tendencies encountered in the outside world correlate with the specific orientation of the conceptually-informed and concept-testing collective activities themselves, and are amenable to the kinds of change those activities seek to induce.

At the limit, then, it would seem that nomad science ends up imperceptibly shading over into philosophy as Deleuze & Guattari define and practice it, in a very apt double-becoming of the one with the other—especially given the fact that the book sets out, as I said at the outset, to "make metaphysics into the correlate for modern science, exactly as modern science is the correlate of a potential metaphysics." But at the same time, it gives Deleuze & Guattari's entire philosophical endeavor a distinctly pragmatic cast, for its fundamental orientation is just as pragmatic as nomad science's is, as we will see in the next section.

So what do these plateaus contribute to the overall project of *A Thousand Plateaus*? They both present a format and an image of thought for the book itself—rhizomatic, nomad thought operating in smooth space—and contrast it with other, arborescent book-formats and modes of thought—State reason and science operating to striate space. This contrast prepares the way for subsequent comparisons, including the critical differences between stratification and de-stratification, between territorialization and de-territorialization, and between the plane of consistency and the plane of organization, to which I will turn in the next section.

ONTO-AESTHETICS

The Problem: How can the Cosmos and Life within it exist in such a way that they are the result of change yet also be always susceptible to further change? How can we understand being in terms of becoming, in terms of difference rather than identity, as a function of the dynamics of open systems? Most importantly, what is the payoff of understanding the world this way? How does it improve our prospects for social change?

The Primary Sources: the Geology of Morals plateau and the Refrain plateau

As we saw in the previous chapter, Deleuze & Guattari understand the real world to encompass both virtual conditions of existence and actual existence, and they construe the realm of the virtual as an open-ended set of Problems to which actual existence is a set of temporary or meta-stable Solutions. Another way of putting this is to say that the Problems of the chaosmos **express** themselves in a set of diverse Solutions, without those contingent Solutions ever exhausting the potential of the chaosmos to actualize or express itself differently. Contingent Solutions are all that are given (in being), from which Problems can be inferred, and yet in a sense it is the Problems that are primary, because it is they that give rise to and express themselves in the various Solutions in the first place. If, as I suggested in the preceding chapter, the fundamental question of Deleuze & Guattari's philosophy is not the definitive "What is it?" but an open-ended "What can become of it?," then there would seem to be no place for ontology. Indeed, the Rhizome plateau ends with praise for American and English literature's ability to use the rhizomatic "logic of the AND [to] overthrow ontology" [25]. In this light, "onto-aesthetics" appears to be the better term. Matter expresses itself in the contingent actualization of Solutions to Problems, and there is no being for Deleuze & Guattari other than those expressions and what gets expressed in them. The key notion of "mutual presupposition," as we will see, prevents any simple distinction from being drawn between expressions and what they express: neither one "comes first," in the same way that neither Problems nor their Solutions "come first": one is expressed in the other; they mutually presuppose one another.

Onto-aesthetics is an apt designation for the issue of expression following the overthrow of ontology in three senses. First of all, it signals the transformation and hybridization of established philosophical fields that is characteristic of the way Deleuze & Guattari practice philosophy: thought picks up speed *au milieu*, in-between. As we saw in the preceding section, epistemology considered within a philosophical perspective that is basically pragmatic in orientation very quickly bleeds over into ethics and politics—and the same will be true for ontology and aesthetics. As if to eliminate any doubts on the subject, Deleuze & Guattari even declare at one point that "politics precedes being" [203]: this is so because any Solution to a given Problem will have been "brought into being" (actualized) by social and technical machines operating in an assemblage whose constitution and operation were inherently political **before** the Solution itself ever emerged. Secondly, aesthetic judgments are just as appropriate as ethical and political ones for assessing Solutions to Problems: mountains and diamonds both express Solutions to the Problem of tectonic pressure, and both are amenable to aesthetic evaluation, even if in very different ways (as Kant's discussion of the relation of the sublime to beauty makes clear). More generally, judgments about the "beauty" or "elegance" of the response embodied in a particular Solution to a Problem abound not just in mathematics and logic, but in architecture and evolutionary biology as well. Characteristically, Deleuze & Guattari place such judgments in these fields on a continuum of variation with judgments in more predictably "aesthetic" fields such as fine art or music. But these fields themselves, finally, where the category "aesthetics" seems most at home, are shown to be developments or off-shoots of a long-term process that increases the autonomy of expression relative to presupposed content throughout both the organic and the alloplastic strata, as we will see below. Aesthetics in this narrow sense really does emerge from an ontology that already entailed the development of an aesthetics in the broader sense, which it is the intention of the term "onto-aesthetics" to express.

"The Geology of Morals—(Who Does The Earth Think It Is?)"

The first thing to note about the Geology plateau is that it is staged from start to finish as a lecture by a science-fiction character named Professor Challenger from a story called "Lost World" by Arthur Conan Doyle! This plateau thus employs one of Deleuze's favorite stylistic techniques: free indirect discourse—with the desired result that it is impossible to tell who is speaking and thus responsible for the content of what is being said: the authors of the plateau, or the lecturer in the plateau. Adopting this dramatic strategy of indirection saves Deleuze & Guattari from a certain embarrassment, or rather enables them to joke their way out of a certain embarrassment: they are writing a book of philosophy, of "pure metaphysics" as Deleuze once characterized it, but here they appear to be doing science, that is to say, explaining how the world works, drawing mostly on the disciplines of geology, chemistry and biology. What they are really doing, however, is extracting philosophically-created concepts (that are hopefully useful) from scientifically-constructed states of affairs (that are hopefully accurate). And the point of doing so is to construe the world in such a way as to make it maximally susceptible to change, with the value of the concepts created being determined pragmatically by the degree to which they enable us to produce desirable change through "real-life operations" in the real world, as we saw in the preceding section on epistemology.

Strata, stratification, de-stratification

The main concept being created in the Geology plateau is **strata**, yielding an account of the processes of stratification and de-stratification. Assemblages and milieus of various kinds are also introduced as components of the concept of strata, with abstract machines driving the processes of both stratification and de-stratification. Finally, the entire process of stratification/de-stratification takes place between two planes: the plane of consistency and the plane of organization (also called the Planomenon and the Ecumenon, respectively). If, as I said earlier, the plane of consistency (Planomenon) consists of the infinite yet determinate sum total of all the virtual potential in the chaosmos, in other words of all possible becomings, the Ecumenon is the sum total of all existing stratifications, the actualization or consolidation of being in a metastable state from out of the chaos of becoming. On principle—the principle of the Eternal Return, and of open systems—being has no ultimate stable state, only an indeterminate number of metastable states: otherwise, the cosmos would have long since reached that state, and would no longer be an open-ended chaosmos. Being is temporary and derivative—and derives, indeed, from becoming. In other words, the consolidation of being out of the amorphous soup of becomings requires thickening agents: coding and territorialization are such agents, and they operate by the process that Deleuze & Guattari—or is it Professor Challenger? or the "Danish Spinozist geologist, Hjelmslev, that dark prince descended from Hamlet," to whom the professor attributes its discovery [43]?—that **someone** calls "double-articulation."

However mistaken Professor Challenger may have been about Hjelmslev being a geologist, Deleuze & Guattari know perfectly well that he was a Danish linguist, not a geologist, and the concept of double-articulation indeed comes to them from linguistics—from the French linguist André Martinet, in fact, but by way of his Danish counterpart, Hjelmslev, who developed a quadripartite schema to replace the binary system of signifier-and-signified bequeathed them by the Swiss linguist Ferdinand de Saussure. Hjelmslev renames signifier and signified "expression" and "content," and crucially adds that each of these two elements is itself articulated or composed of both form and substance: the first articulation correlates form and substance of content; the second correlates form and substance of expression. Hjelmslev also adds a fifth term, which—because, unlike Saussure, he maintained a communicational framework for his linguistics—he called matter or "purport": that is, the sense that the double-articulation of content and expression was intended to convey. In extending Hjelmslev's quadripartite schema beyond linguistics to the chaosmos as whole, Deleuze & Guattari substitute the plane of consistency for Hjelmslev's matter, as their counterpart to his fifth term: double-articulation is the abstract machine that consolidates being in strata of all kinds by coding and territorializing the unformed and non-localized matter of the plane of consistency. Matter can thus be said to express or self-organize itself via double-articulation throughout the chaosmos. Indeed, one reason to call double-articulation an **abstract** machine is precisely to underscore how consistently it operates in a wide range of fields: not only linguistics, but also geology, chemistry, biology, and so forth.

The other key component that Deleuze & Guattari adopt from Hjelmslev's linguistics is his characterization of the relation between content and expression as one of reciprocal presupposition. As I have said, neither content nor expression has causal precedence over the other; they simply presuppose one another. To put the point another way, the reciprocal presupposition of content and expression maintains the immanence of self-organization in an open system: neither term in the relation can convert to precedence and transcendence. Among its many advantages as an account of the derivation-consolidation of being from the plane of becomings, this formulation has two distinct polemical targets: orthodox Lacanianism and orthodox Marxism. The privilege

Lacan assigns (against the grain of Saussure's original understanding) to the signifier over the signified is well-known; Deleuze & Guattari diagnose this privileging as the hallmark of despotism in *Anti-Oedipus*: a certain power-structure with its specific regime of signs converts reciprocal presupposition into the hierarchical precedence of one term over the other. Only by maintaining reciprocal presupposition as a given can this despotism of the signifier be diagnosed, in the particular social formations that organize signification in this way, as well as in the discourse and practice of psychoanalysis [67]. Orthodox Marxism, meanwhile, makes the converse mistake: it considers content to be determinate (even if only "in the last instance") and relegates expression to the status of mere "superstructure," often with a first floor constituted by a State apparatus and above that a second floor comprised of ideology [68]. Privileging the economic base obscures the variable correlations between the State-form and production-exchange relations at the moments of emergence, consolidation and globalization of capitalism and other modes of production. In order to maintain the immanence of self-organization, a mode of production must be understood as the contingent result of machinic processes of double-articulation (as Deleuze & Guattari will insist later, in the Capture plateau [435]), not as a unified totality determining hierarchized articulations in advance.

To sum up what has been said so far, the concept of stratification is extracted from the dynamics of the chaosmos as explained by the contemporary sciences that draw on non-linear mathematics and complexity theory (among other sources). Crucial to these sciences is the category of "emergence," along with the associated notion of irreversible time. From phenomena of emergence in a wide range of fields, Deleuze & Guattari extract a concept of immanent self-organization, and furthermore specify a mechanism by which such self-organization or stratification is often accomplished: a double-articulation involving both forms and substances of content and of expression, with content and expression co-existing in reciprocal presupposition.

Deleuze & Guattari present Foucault's study of the modern prison as an exemplary analysis of stratification through double-articulation. Foucault's analysis hinges on the relation between what he calls the "seeable" and the "sayable"—but this relation is crucially **not** a relation of signification whereby the sayable would be the signifier of the seeable as signified. Instead of two terms, there are four: the prison as stratum is neither a thing nor a signified, but rather a form of content, the "prison-form" or modern prison design, coupled with specific substance of content: bodies, organs (particularly eyes), buildings, power relations. The correlative expression of the prison stratum is not the signifier "prison," but an entire discourse (or "discursive formation") on "delinquency" and "corrective punishment," coupled with specific substance of expression including legislative acts, policy statements, juridical sentences and so forth. What's more, content and expression were not born together in one stroke: prison design and the discourse of delinquency each has its own separate history or derivation, and they eventually fall into a relation of reciprocal presupposition almost as if by chance. It is only in subsequent works that Foucault reduces the factor of chance in the emergence of the prison-delinquency complex by situating it as one stratum among several in the context of a new paradigm of social relations he will call disciplinary power.

Deleuze & Guattari, meanwhile, will call disciplinary power an abstract machine—a machine that is abstract, once again, because a number of other institutions or strata share it, including schools, barracks, hospitals, factories, and so on [67]. Indeed, the process of double-articulation composing a given stratum never takes place in a vacuum: it presupposes what Deleuze & Guattari call "parastrata" co-existing alongside it, with which it shares either forms or substances or both. Thus the prison stratum co-exists in reciprocal presupposition with the judicial stratum: neither one causes the other, but they are inconceivable and totally impracticable without one another. Parastrata thus form a "horizontal" network of reciprocal presupposition in which one stratum serves as a parastratum for others that serve as parastrata for it, and vice versa. What counts as a stratum or a parastratum is entirely arbitrary or relative. And the same is true for what Deleuze & Guattari call "epistrata," which "pile one atop the other" in a kind of "vertical" meshwork or chain. I said that the expression of the prison-delinquency complex is not the words "prison" or "delinquency," but an entire discursive formation on delinquency. But of course the statements comprising that discursive formation are indeed composed of sentences and words, the latter of which are themselves composed of morphemes and phonemes. The prison stratum thus presupposes the epistratum of French or English, which in turn presupposes the epistratum of a language-capable species, which in turn presupposes a whole set of biological, physiological, chemical and physical epistrata, and so on. "A stratum exists only in its epistrata and parastrata," Deleuze & Guattari explain, and "in the final analysis these must be considered strata in their own right" [52]. So it's parastrata all around, and epistrata all the way down, "each stratum serving as the substratum for another stratum" [72]—until we reach the plane of consistency, that is: and the "first" stratum to emerge from the plane of consistency, so to speak, Deleuze & Guattari call a "metastratum." But of course there is no "first" stratum; the Ecumenon is nothing like the Great Chain of Being.[6] All strata presuppose co-existing parastrata, which means that none can be first; and at the same time, all strata presuppose and derive ultimately from the plane of consistency, however indirectly. Deleuze & Guattari are adamant to rule out any hint of perfectionism, progressivism, or evolutionism from their account of stratification:

> It is difficult to elucidate the system of the strata without seeming to introduce a kind of cosmic or spiritual evolution from one to the other, as if they were arranged in stages and ascended degrees of perfection. Nothing of the sort. [...] There is no biosphere or noosphere, but everywhere the same Mecanosphere. If one begins by considering the strata in themselves, it cannot be said that one is less organized that another. This even applies to a stratum serving as substratum: there is no fixed order, and one stratum can serve directly as a substratum for another without the intermediaries one [might] expect there to be from the standpoint of stages and degrees (for example, microphysical sectors can serve as an immediate substratum for organic phenomena). Or the apparent order can be reversed, with cultural or technical phenomena providing a fertile soil, a good soup, for the development of insects, bacteria, germs, or even particles. The industrial age defined as the age of insects... It's even worse nowadays: you can't even tell in advance which stratum is going to communicate with which other, or in what direction. Above all, there is no lesser, no higher or lower, organization; the substratum is an integral part of the stratum, is bound up with it as the milieu in which change occurs, [but] not an increase in organization. [69]

This principle of parity among strata, substrata, parastrata and epistrata is extremely important, for among other reasons as a safeguard against transcendence. And this is particularly so in light of the distinction Deleuze & Guattari make among the "three major types of strata" [64] which I am calling "mega-strata": the inorganic, the organic and the alloplastic. These mega-strata are to be distinguished not in terms of their levels of complexity or degrees of organization, but rather in terms of the distinctive mode of double-articulation that characterizes each of them, and it is to these that I will turn shortly.

Milieus, assemblages, territories

Before doing so, however, I will need to examine a set of terms employed by Deleuze & Guattari, here and in several other plateaus, that are closely related to strata: milieus, assemblages, and territories. Milieus are the material environments (consisting of matter and energy flows) in which strata and territories are formed, and they are divided into several sub-categories. We have seen that a given stratum may serve as a substratum for another stratum; in doing so, the substratum furnishes the stratum with molecular materials that thereby get transformed into substantial elements of the stratum in question. (It should be noted that these molecular materials "are not the same as the unformed matter of the plane of consistency; they are already stratified," since they come from a substratum [49].) Such a substratum is considered the "exterior milieu" of the stratum in question. Its "interior milieu" is composed of those same substantial elements articulated with the formal relations that transformed them from the materials furnished by the exterior milieu. So for example a super-saturated solution serves as the exterior milieu for a stratum of crystal, as the molecular materials in liquid form get transformed into a solid in the process of crystallization comprising the interior milieu. Similarly on the organic mega-stratum, the "prebiotic soup" [49] of elements necessary for the emergence of life serves as an exterior milieu, with chemical catalysts acting as the correlate of seed crystals in the composition of the interior milieu of a living organism. Thirdly, there are "associated milieus" composed of factors that contribute to the existence a stratum without becoming part of it: gravity and mammalian sweat are crucial factors in the associated milieu of the tick, for example, as its olfactory sense produces a release response that then allows gravity to bring it into contact with the skin or hide, where a grab response will in turn give it access to the material of its exterior milieu which it will ingest, namely blood; mammalian blood forms part of the tick's exterior milieu, while sweat is part of its associated milieu. Finally, Deleuze & Guattari mention another type of milieu, called "intermediary milieus," which are here strictly synonymous with epistrata and parastrata [52] (but receive further elaboration in the Refrain plateau, where they usually take the form of membranes). The plane of consistency is the milieu of all milieus.

Assemblages, also called "concrete machinic assemblages" [71], are the actual agents of self-organization of the process of stratification: they are located simultaneously at the intersection of contents and expression on a given stratum, at the intersections among various strata (also known then as "interstrata"), and at the intersection of any stratum with the plane of consistency (then also called a "metastratum") [73]. Concrete machinic assemblages are also the means by which abstract machines get effectuated in the strata, and thus the Mechanosphere can be understood as a sub-set or outgrowth of the plane of consistency: not the sum total of all **possible** becomings, but "the set of all [**actualized**] abstract machines and machinic assemblages [whether located] outside the strata, on the strata, or between strata" [71]. Since concrete assemblages are situated between the strata and the plane of consistency, they are vectors both of stratification, in relation to the plane of consistency on which they draw for matter and energy to form or consolidate the strata, and of de-stratification, in relation to the strata they are able to transform by drawing on and assembling different matter-energy flows from the plane of consistency. Territories, finally, are machinic assemblages belonging to the alloplastic mega-stratum. Deleuze & Guattari even go so far as to claim that "the territory is the first assemblage" [323], even though in the Rhizome and Geology plateaus the term assemblage has a far broader range of application. In any case, territorial assemblage marks an important threshold between the organic and the alloplastic mega-strata, as we will see below and in connection with the Refrain plateau.

Finally, there are the terms "molar" and "molecular," which play an important role in both *Anti-Oedipus* and *A Thousand*

Plateaus. There are several ways of approaching the relations between molar and molecular. One is in connection with the articulation of content and expression. As we have seen, a substance can take liquid form on the molecular level, and then get transformed into a crystal on the molar level: water vapor becomes a snowflake. Notice that molecular and molar are relative terms: when individual snowflakes combine to form a snowdrift, or a snowman, it is now the snowflakes that constitute the molecular level, while the snowdrift and snowman are molar. Notice, too, that the molar form taken by an aggregate of millions of snowflakes can be intentional (snowman) or purely statistical (snowdrift): the term "molar" derives from the very large number of particles required to treat a given aggregate in terms of probability, inasmuch as the deviant behavior of any single particle—no matter how aberrant—gets damped out by the average behavior of the rest. The recourse to statistical probabilities may be what gives rise to the false impression that the difference between molar and molecular is a matter of size, when in fact it is more a matter of perspective: relative to water-vapor molecules, the snowflake crystal remains molar, despite its very small size. Finally, molecular and molar differ as to the type of order involved, corresponding generally to the difference between the plane of consistency (the Planomenon), which is molecular and the plane of organization (the Ecumenon), which is molar.

Mega-strata

Returning now to the three "major types of strata" [64] or mega-strata, it must be said that although they don't exhibit a progression in levels of complexity or degrees of organization, their respective modes of double-articulation do exhibit a progression in one other respect: **expression becomes increasingly autonomous from the content it presupposes**, with a corresponding increase in powers of de-territorialization. This key development, as I said, is one reason for the neologism "onto-aesthetics." On the inorganic stratum, expression and content occupy the same milieu; stratification transforms molecular materials into molar substances, and the degree of de-territorialization is relatively small. In the process of crystallization, for instance, it is the same chemical elements that are transformed from liquid to solid state, and de-territorialization can take place only at the edges of the crystal and only when the surrounding medium is sufficiently saturated; such a stratum can expand in its immediately contiguous vicinity, but it cannot reproduce itself. The development of strata on the inorganic mega-stratum occurs via what Deleuze & Guattari call "inductions," with the inducing expression and the induced content occupying the same medium. The organic mega-stratum, by contrast, stratifies via "transductions," where expression has become linear and independent: it now takes the form of the genetic code. Populations or species can also expand (like crystals), but their expansion is not necessarily limited to the immediate vicinity, and is almost always made possible by the capacity of members or pairs of the species to reproduce themselves. Most important, the coefficient of de-territorialization on the organic stratum has increased exponentially, due to phenomena such as random mutation and genetic drift. I will return to examine the mode of double-articulation of the organic stratum further in connection with the Refrain plateau.

The coefficient of de-territorialization exponentially increases yet again on the alloplastic stratum: here, the spatial linearity of the genetic code is superseded by the temporal linearity of the linguistic code, and this form of expression has become even more independent of the contents it presupposes. Indeed, Deleuze & Guattari call this mode of double-articulation "translation," in order to highlight not just "the ability of one language to 'represent' in some way the givens of another language, but beyond that... the ability of language [itself], with its own givens on its own stratum, to represent all the other strata and thus achieve a scientific conception of the world" [62]. At the same time that the form of expression becomes linguistic, and hence is subject to modification from the outside (unlike the genetic code, until recently), the technological elaboration of forms of content facilitates the modification of the external world. The double-articulation of the third mega-stratum thus correlates technologies (as content) with symbols (as expression)—as we saw in the case of Foucault's exemplary analysis of the social technology of incarceration and the discursive formation of delinquency. Speaking more generally, Deleuze & Guattari insist that "content should be understood not simply as the hand and [specific] tools, but as a technical social machine that preexists them and constitutes states of force or formations of power [just as] expression should be understood not simply as the face and language... but as a semiotic collective machine that preexists them and constitutes regimes of signs" [63]. Because its form of expression (language) enables the "universal translation" [63] of all other strata and its form of content (technology) enables the alloplastic modification of nearly anything in the external world [60], the third stratum harbors immense and increasingly complex technical and semiotic machines that "rear up and stretch their pincers out in all directions at all the other strata," as Deleuze & Guattari put it (or is this Professor Challenger speaking?). Looking beyond the Geology plateau for a moment, I would say that capitalism is foremost among such machines: we will see that its process of axiomatization operates transversally to most strata and operates directly on de-coded and de-territorialized flows of matter and energy at a minimum remove from the plane of consistency. For the time being, however, suffice it to say that the great technical-semiotic machines of the third stratum produce what Deleuze & Guattari call "the illusion constitutive of man" [63]: "who does man think he is?" they ask in ironic echo of the plateau's subtitle, "(Who Does the Earth Think It Is?)." Yet the kind of "stratoanalysis" [43] for which the Geology plateau lays the groundwork is intended to (among other things) debunk this illusion by showing for one thing that the alloplastic stratum does not belong exclusively to the human species, and for another, that what humans do accomplish on this stratum depends on forces that are not necessarily under human control—but all this only becomes clear in other plateaus, including the Refrain plateau. So it must be said that while the Geology plateau covers a lot of ground—practically the entire cosmos, from the sub-atomic level to complex cutting-edge technologies and social formations—its immediate pay-off is ultimately rather slim. Perhaps that is why at the end of his lecture, "no one tried to keep Professor Challenger from leaving, [as he], or what remained of him, slowly hurried toward the *plane of consistency*" [73]. But this plateau does establish a conceptual framework for the contributions and polemics of other plateaus—most notably the Refrain plateau, to which I turn next.

"On the Refrain"

Although they are separated by seven other plateaus (half the book!), in a sense the Refrain plateau picks right up where the Geology plateau left off, exploring in further detail the alloplastic stratum as it emerges from the organic stratum, and further developing the concepts of milieu and territory. It should also be said, however, that the Refrain plateau builds directly on the final "becoming-music" section of the immediately-preceding Becomings plateau, too. (Such is the nature of a rhizome-book, and the attendant challenges of navigating one.) Finally, and this is one of its important pay-offs, the Refrain plateau provides a crucial hinge between Deleuze & Guattari's onto-aesthetics and what I will call their "anthro-ethology" in the next section. Earlier I characterized this "anthropology" as structuralist and anti-humanist. One aspect of its anti-humanism is a familiar precept of structuralism: human beings are over-determined by the Symbolic order; we are not masters in our own house. And indeed Deleuze & Guattari will have much to say about language, money, and the image of the face as determining components of the Symbolic order. The other aspect of their anti-humanism is less familiar, and far more interesting: human being and human behavior—and aesthetics in particular—are placed on a continuum with those of other animals. It is in this light that Deleuze & Guattari's anti-humanist "anthropology" is best understood as a hybrid ethological-anthropology or "anthro-ethology"—and it is the Refrain plateau that contributes much (though not all) of the ethology to the mix.

Rhythm, milieu, territory

As is perhaps inevitable, a certain amount of terminological groundwork must be established for the philosophical payoff of the concept of the refrain to become clear—even if the plateau itself starts with a wonderful account (derived in part from Paul Klee's theory of painting!) of how children and housewives (among others) use refrains first to establish and then eventually to break free of protective territories (their "comfort zones," so to speak). Taking up the two concepts of milieu and territory developed earlier in the book, Deleuze & Guattari now add the concept of rhythm, inserted between the two: rhythm arises in the relation between two milieus—and this relation is one of difference. "A milieu is a block of space-time constituted by the periodic repetition of [a milieu-component]," and the milieu is coded by that periodic repetition [313]. But milieus as organic strata don't exist in a vacuum any more than inorganic strata do; rather, one milieu will serve as the milieu of another milieu, much as any given stratum can serve as the substratum or parastratum for another stratum. Thus each milieu-code "is in a perpetual state of transcoding or transduction" [313]—transduction, as we have seen, being the hallmark of the organic mega-stratum: transduction, Deleuze & Guattari explain, "is the manner in which one milieu serves as the basis for another, or... is established atop another milieu, [or] dissipates in it or is constituted in it" [313]. And it is transduction that introduces rhythm into the organic stratum.

Rhythm is utterly distinct from meter (in the same way that smooth space can be distinguished from striated): meter involves a measured, homogenous repetition of the same (the same interval of time) **within** a milieu, whereas rhythm is "the Unequal or... Incommensurable" relation of difference **between** milieus. "Meter is dogmatic," as Deleuze & Guattari put it, "but rhythm is critical: it ties together critical moments, or ties itself together in passing from one milieu to another" [313]. The wing-span and flapping tempo of a fly are metrical, as are the circuits of a spider spinning its web and the dimensions of the resulting mesh: the relations between the two set up a rhythm. "It is as though the spider had a fly in its head," Deleuze & Guattari suggest, or "a fly 'motif' [or] a fly 'refrain' " [314]. In this case the rhythm is predatory (the mesh-span is "designed" to be smaller than the wing-span); in others it is symbiotic, as with snapdragons and bumblebees, orchids and wasps. In their complex networks of relations with the surrounding environment, milieu components (such as wing-span or mesh-size) become "melodies in counterpoint, each of which serves as a motif for another: Nature as music" [314], as Deleuze & Guattari say, citing the work of German biologist and animal-behavior specialist Jakob von Uexküll. So far, then, the organic mega-stratum appears as a vast synchronic or symphonic structure of rhythmic differences, melodies, motifs and counterpoints. But we don't yet have territories. Territoriality belongs only to certain animals, as yet another way of addressing the Intra-Species Social Organization Problem.

The crucial threshold of territoriality is reached within the organic stratum when milieu components and/or rhythmic motifs cease to be merely functional (e.g., predatory or symbiotic) and become **expressive** instead. And what they express first and foremost is territoriality itself: components and motifs cease being functional and become the marks or indexes of territory.

> Take the example of color in birds or fish: color is a membrane state associated with interior hormonal states, but it remains functional and transitory as long as it is tied to a type of action (sexuality, aggressiveness, flight). It becomes expressive, [by contrast], when it acquires a temporal constancy and a spatial range that make it a territorial, or rather a territorializing, mark. [315]

The territorialization threshold can be very difficult to discern; it can even pass between different populations of a single species of bird, as when the species contains both colored and uncolored members, and the colored ones have a territory while the uncolored ones are gregarious and do not: color serves no purpose here other than to mark territory [315]. In a similar vein, a given rhythmic function may be re-purposed when it is part of a territorial assemblage: aggressive impulses, for example, take on different or additional functions for a territorial animal, inasmuch as they can be directed against members of its own species, whereas with predatory animals they are functionally directed against their prey. (Of course, nothing says a species can't be both territorial and predatory.) The essential thing is that specifically territorial aggression has become **expressive**, expressive of territory—and no longer has anything directly to do with the need for nourishment, for example; indeed it usually no longer even entails killing (unlike predatory aggression, which always does).

We have seen that the hallmark of the organic stratum relative to the inorganic was the displacement of the organizing plane of expression onto the genetic code, which thereby became independent of the plane of content it organizes. Territorialization takes a further step in the same direction: past this new threshold, milieu components and rhythmic motifs become independent of their erstwhile conditions or functions, and become expressive of territory instead; they enter into territorial refrains. Paradoxically enough, territorialization thus entails a certain de-coding: components and motifs must be released from functional roles in order to become expressive. What's more, territorializing marks may themselves be subject to de-territorialization, as when elements of a territorial assemblage get released from territorial expression in order to serve a different form of expression—as part of a courtship assemblage in the presence of a female when the male has elevated mating hormone levels, for instance. The independence of expression from presupposed content becomes more and more pronounced. In the same vein, as territorial (and other) refrains develop, the expressive traits comprising them enter into increasingly complex relations with one another, independent of the internal impulses (such as sex or aggression) and external circumstances (presence of a mate or a rival) they express. Deleuze & Guattari call these complexes "territorial motifs" when they involve the impulses of a territory's interior milieu, and "territorial counterpoints" when they involve the circumstances of its exterior milieu. The result of the increasing complexity of expression is that these motifs and counterpoints end up expressing the **relation** of the territory **to** those impulses and circumstances rather than directly expressing the impulses and circumstances themselves—another **increase in the autonomy of expression**.

> Expressive qualities entertain variable or constant relations with one another (that is what matters of expression *do);* they no longer constitute [mere indexes] that mark a territory, but motifs and counterpoints that express the **relation** of the territory to interior impulses or exterior circumstances, **whether or not they are given**. [318; my emphasis]

Eventually, expressive elements may become practically independent of functional content, impulses and circumstances altogether, as when a courtship song is sung in the absence of a female of the species; or when a territorial refrain is sung in the absence of a rival; or when a mockingbird sings in accompaniment to someone playing the piano, for no particular reason. In this regard, Deleuze & Guattari are critical of ethologists who characterize this growing autonomy of expression in terms of "ritualization," even though this term does capture the repetitive quality of a behavior detached from the immediacy of impulses and circumstances; but in their view, what the relative freedom from a direct relation to presupposed content in expressive motifs and counterpoints in fact enables is an exploration of the potentialities of the interior and exterior milieus, without actually altering or engaging the milieus themselves [318]. (The first light of **access to the virtual** dawns, well in advance of even the cub's-play of wolves.)

"Art does not wait for human beings to begin"

And now for the pay-off of all the time and energy invested in the careful categorical distinctions and nuanced terminology of Deleuze & Guattari's aesthetic ontology: "art does not wait for human beings to begin" [320]—and perhaps even more important, art takes precedence over "instinct"—even in animals. "Can the [becoming-expressive of rhythm and territorial motifs] be called Art?"—Deleuze & Guattari ask? And their answer is yes. Even the simplest of "territorial marks are readymades," they insist: you can "take anything and make it a matter of expression" [316], as the stagemaker bird does "each morning by dropping leaves it picks from its tree, and then [carefully] turning them [over] so the paler underside stands out against the dirt" [315]. Deleuze & Guattari prefer ethology—the study of animal behavior—to ethnology—the study of only human groups and characteristics—because the human species shares with other animals, and in an evolutionary sense derives from other animals, this predisposition to make art and to territorialize, as I will show in more detail in a moment.

But even within ethology, there is a polemic to be waged against models of behavior that entail reductive binary oppositions or exclusive disjunctions—such as the categorization of animal behaviors as either acquired or innate. For in territorial assemblages, as we have seen, milieu components that were functional or subject to the periodic-coded repetition of instinct get de-coded in order to serve as territorial markers, and then territorial motifs and counterpoints achieve yet another significant degree of autonomy from their interior and exterior milieus. "From the moment there is a territorial assemblage," Deleuze & Guattari explain, the innate assumes a very particular figure, since it is inseparable from a movement of decoding [and therefore] quite unlike the [impulsive or instinctual] innate of the interior milieu; acquisition also assumes a very particular figure, since it is... regulated by matters of expression rather than by stimuli in the exterior milieu. [332]

The territorial assemblage, they conclude, simultaneously entails "a decoding of innateness and a territorialization of learning" [332]. Distinct groups of a single species of sparrow living in different areas of New York's Central Park provide a perfect illustration: they are as a species genetically equipped to sing, and instinctually predisposed to sing territorial refrains, but the refrains sung by specific sparrows vary slightly depending on where they live and which territorial group they belong to: instinct has been decoded and acquisition has been territorialized, in what can only be called a form of "sparrow multiculturalism."

But that's not all. Territorialization is a way of addressing the Intra-Species Social Organization Problem, for humans and other animal species alike: territory establishes a critical distance among members of the same species. Just as animal territories "ensure and regulate the coexistence of members of the same species by keeping them apart" [320], so do sales territories ensure and regulate the coexistence of members of the same company's marketing department by keeping **them** apart. At the same time, Deleuze & Guattari suggest, territorialization "makes possible the coexistence of a maximum number of species in the same milieu by specializing them" [320], just as territorial specialization enables salespeople to coexist with engineers, drill-press operators, and other specialists in the same company—and, on a larger scale, it enables a company specializing in one product or service to coexist with companies occupying what are tellingly called other "market niches." "In animals as in human beings," Deleuze & Guattari conclude,

> there are rules of critical distance for competition: [...] a territorialization of functions is the condition for their emergence as "occupations" or "trades." Thus intraspecific or specialized aggressiveness is necessarily a territorialized aggressiveness; it does not explain the territory [but rather] derives from it. [And

in fact, art is the] territorializing factor that is the necessary condition for the emergence of the work-function. [321]

In this way, supposedly human institutions, such as specialization and the division of labor, are shown to exist on a continuum with the "institutions" or behavior-patterns of other animal species. Returning for a moment to the modern prison analyzed by Foucault, we can now understand the articulation (of the seeable and the sayable), of expression and content, of institutional discourses and practices, as more than a relation of mutual presupposition: that relation itself is the result of a territorialization.

But critical distance is not the only Solution to the ISSO Problem proposed by territorializing assemblages. For they can produce not only a reorganization of functions (e.g., specialization) but also a regrouping and intensification of forces. Here, I will treat this Solution only briefly, since Emile Durkheim has devoted an entire book to this phenomenon in humans, his *Elementary Forms of Religious Life*. Members of a species that ordinarily live in isolation from one another (whether in rival territories or not) sometimes gather together in large numbers to form a gregarious territory: hermit crabs do this in order to exchange shells; spiny lobsters form long marching-columns (a kind of mobile territory) in order to escape into deeper water from storm-season sub-surface turbulence. Both the shell-exchange refrain and the long-march refrain share a feature common to all territories, rival or gregarious: they offer protection. But the lobster refrain shares a different feature with the refrains of many species of migratory birds and cycling pelotons: the energy-saving aerodynamics of traveling in slipstreams. In line with Durkheim (whom they don't mention in this connection, however), Deleuze & Guattari consider religions to operate as gregarious territories as well: even among groups who usually live apart, religions bring people together in territories organized around a special territorializing mark or symbol (a totem animal, a totem sign like a cross, a totemic person such as a god, etc.), and that territorialization produces a regrouping and intensification of force which is then attributed to the territory or to its totem figure. "So we must once again acknowledge," Deleuze & Guattari conclude, "that religion, which is common to human beings and animals, occupies territory only because it depends on … [a] territorializing factor as its necessary condition" [321], and that "this factor... at the same time organizes the functions of the milieu into occupations and binds the forces of chaos in rites and religions" [322]. Needless to say, religious refrains can and should be understood as precursors to national or nationalism refrains—of which national anthems themselves are merely the most blatant and narrowly musical of instances. It should also be noted, if only in passing, that the regrouping and intensification of force attendant on territorialization can lead to fascism as well as religion [348, 299–301].

Refrains and music

Deleuze & Guattari end up classifying refrains into three main types [326-7]: (1) rudimentary territorial refrains that simply mark and assemble a territory; (2) territorialized refrains that assume a specialized function within an assemblage (e.g. professional refrains territorializing trades and occupations), but can also transfer to other assemblages (as when a territorial motif transfers into a courtship assemblage); and finally (3) refrains that regroup and intensify forces, either to strengthen a territory or to leave it behind and travel elsewhere. With the mention of national anthems, however, we have almost imperceptibly crossed another threshold—this time from the refrain into music itself. And once again, the threshold is difficult to discern with any precision; it certainly doesn't correspond to the animal-human divide, because on one hand, many birds are certainly musicians [301], and on the other hand, even many human "refrains"—in Deleuze & Guattari's ethological sense: professional refrains, for example—are not musical at all. What's more, some human music (such as the national anthem) is more refrain-like than the music of some song-birds (such as the mockingbird). The threshold is nevertheless a crucial one, because the vocation of music according to Deleuze & Guattari is ultimately to **de-territorialize the refrain**. This is the culmination of a long process crossing a number of thresholds, as we have seen, each one involving an **increase in the autonomy of expression** in relation to presupposed content: rhythms developed through the transcoding of milieus connected with other milieus; territory itself was initially constituted by the de-coding of milieus and milieu-functions; territorialized functions were in turn de-territorialized in their passage into or connection with other assemblages, and in the development of increasingly autonomous territorial motifs and counterpoints out of internal impulses and external circumstances. Eventually, we arrive at what I am tempted to call **pure music**—at the direct connection of a completely de-territorialized musical plane of expression with the forces of the cosmos at large. Accounting for this trajectory explains the—perhaps surprising—appearance toward the end of the plateau of a set of "summary definitions" of Classicism, Romanticism and Modernism in Western art-music. Significantly, this tripartite partition of musical forms roughly follows the tripartite classification of refrain-types discussed above [326–7]. Classicism is thus presented as preparation for the establishment of territory, through the constitution of milieus and the imposition of form on matter: "What the artist confronts... is chaos, the forces of chaos, the forces of raw and untamed matter upon which Forms must be imposed in order to make substances, and Codes in order to make milieus" [338]. Romanticism, in turn, is described as a turning away from classical universalism in the establishment of territories, with all their particularities: "the artist territorializes, enters a territorial assemblage" [338]. Here, the artist no longer confronts the forces of chaos, but tries to manage the forces of the Earth and invoke the forces of a People, even if the territory is lost and the people are missing. The Modern age, finally, is described as "the age of the cosmic": here, music "no longer confronts the forces of chaos, it no longer uses the forces of the earth or the people to deepen itself but instead opens onto the forces of the Cosmos" [342]. Without passing through intermediaries of form and content, beyond both territory and refrain, the artist now captures cosmic forces directly with bare sound. Just as for Klee the role of painting was no longer to reproduce the visible but to "render visible," the task of modern music is to render audible the silent forces of the cosmos.

Although this somewhat hasty excursus on Western art-music is the last word of the Refrain plateau in a literal sense, it matches up very directly with the plateau's opening pages, which I find far more suggestive (and where Guattari the therapist may prevail over Deleuze the aesthete of the closing pages). "A child in the dark, gripped with fear, comforts himself by singing under his breath," is how the plateau begins, with a child singing a refrain to comfort himself. This first stage is preliminary to the establishment of a territory: make a mark; find a calm center; tame chaos. The second step is to draw a boundary surrounding that center, to form a protective territory with a refrain: "A child hums to summon the strength for the schoolwork she has to hand in. A housewife sings to herself, or listens to the radio, as she marshals the anti-chaos forces of her work" [311]. The third step, finally, is to go on beyond territory, and get outside:

> Finally, one opens the circle a crack, opens it all the way, lets someone in, calls someone, or else goes out oneself, launches forth. One opens the circle not on the side where the old forces of chaos press against it but in another region, one created by the circle itself. As though the circle tended on its own to open onto a future, as a function of the working forces it shelters. This time, it is in order to join with the forces of the future, cosmic forces. One launches forth, hazards an improvisation. But to improvise is to join with the World, or meld with it. One ventures from home on the thread of a tune. [311]

I find this account particularly suggestive because I take jazz improvisation to be a perfect illustration of nomadism, one of Deleuze & Guattari's most important contributions to political philosophy. But let me also emphasize that the significance of the refrain is that it establishes an ethological and pre- or para-representational basis for Human Intra-Species Social Organization, on a continuum with the ISSO Solutions practiced by other species. The refrain thus serves as substratum for the constitution of the Symbolic Order, where the expression-plane crosses another critical threshold of independence. It is to Deleuze & Guattari's anthro-ethology and the role of the Symbolic Order within it that I turn next.

To sum up what these plateaus contribute to the overall project of *A Thousand Plateaus*: from the starting point of a chaosmos characterized primarily by difference and becoming, they describe processes of stratification (and de-stratification) and territorialization (and de-territorialization) that situate human being in a context of cosmic becoming. In this way, even the most "human" of activities and institutions can be understood on a continuum with processes informing not just other forms of animal life (such as refrains), but the cosmos as a whole. Key to this continuum is the increasing autonomy of expression relative to content as we pass from one mega-stratum to the next—from the inorganic, to the organic, to the alloplastic—and it is on the alloplastic mega-stratum that the Symbolic Order emerges.

ANTHRO-ETHOLOGY

The Problem: How does the human life-form occupy the alloplastic stratum Symbolically; how is human social self-organization accomplished through and reflected in signs—through language, money, and images?

The Primary Sources: "Postulates of Linguistics," "On Several Regimes of Signs," "Faciality," and "Apparatus of Capture"

Already in the Refrain plateau, as we have just seen, human behaviors are considered on par with animal behaviors, and in that sense they fall under the category of "ethology," the study of animal behavior. Yet there is also something distinctive about human behavior: it is mediated not just through territories and refrains, but also through the Symbolic Order or semiotic stratum. For this reason, and because shared animal behaviors such as territorialization serve as a key substratum for even those human behaviors mediated by the semiotic stratum, the hybrid term "anthro-ethology" can be used to designate the specifically human (or anthropological) portion of the universe of animal behavior (ethology). There are three main elements of the semiotic stratum, and I will examine their contributions to human Intra-Species Social Organization in this order: first language, then what they call "faciality," and finally money.

"Postulates of Linguistics"

As is often the case, Deleuze & Guattari begin their discussion of language with a polemic: the Linguistics plateau identifies and overturns four fundamental postulates that they consider false, all the while drawing on selected contributions from the philosophers of language J. L. Austin and Voloshinov/Bahktin, from structural linguistics, and particularly from the work of Louis Hjelmslev. The four erroneous postulates can be summarized as follows:

I. Language is essentially or primarily informational and communicational

II. Language can and should be understood separately from "extrinsic" factors

III. Language has constants and universals that make it a homogeneous system

IV. Linguistics that is scientific studies only standard or major languages.

We have already seen the importance of Hjelmslev's quadripartite division of signification into form and substance of content combined with form and substance of expression. Less well-known but equally important for Deleuze & Guattari's critique of linguistics is Hjemslev's insertion between the language-system and speech-acts (between Saussure's *langue* and *parole*) of what he called "usage": the sub-set of statements actually pronounced by a given language-community from the infinite set of all statements made possible within the language-system. (The early Foucault developed the concept of usage, albeit without citing Hjelmslev, in theorizing and analyzing what he called discursive formations.) Deleuze & Guattari take this development one step further by adding to the actualized variants of language included in usage the additional potentialities and continuous variation that inhere in language as a virtual structure or system, as we will see.

But first, let's examine their alternative to the view that language essentially involves information and communication. Austin had already identified what he considered a special case of language where statements perform actions by the very fact of being stated—as when a judge or priest says "I now pronounce you husband and wife." Deleuze & Guattari extend this insight to all of language, which is thus re-defined as the set of what they call "order-words." Language's primary function is not to communicate or inform, but to issue orders: "The elementary unit of language is the order-word," they insist, and "information is only the strict minimum necessary for the emission, transmission, and observation of orders as commands" [76]. But commands are only the most obvious instance of order-words: even constative statements (i.e., statements of fact) are order-words in that they impose order on the world, and are accompanied by a command-function that has become implicit: "you shall believe that…"—or better yet: "Let it be said that… ." Because the effect of order-words is not even a matter of belief, much less of truth, but of obedience and conformity, much of which is unconscious.

Notice the grammatical construction of the presupposed constative order-word, "Let it be said that…": there is no subject of the enunciation. This points to the importance of free indirect discourse and the indefinite third person pronoun in Deleuze & Guattari's understanding of language. Rather than the direct communication of information between a first and a second person, language is primarily hearsay, rumor—what "one" supposedly saw, said or did. But even the indefinite pronoun "one" becomes implicit in free indirect discourse, which is attributable to no one: such is the provenance of the constative order-word. Something like this was already a precept of structuralism: we don't speak language, language speaks us. But following Hjelmslev and Foucault, Deleuze & Guattari make this inversion more explicit and specific. It's not language in general that speaks, but rather what they call a "collective assemblage of enunciation," which is always located in a particular place and time and in relation to a machinic assemblage of desire or practice—as we saw in Foucault's analysis of incarceration-technology and delinquency-discourse. Individual statements, if and when they occur, derive from a collective assemblage of enunciation: a judge may end up pronouncing a judicial sentence legitimately, but her statement and its legitimacy depend strictly on its precise position within the collective assemblage of enunciation. In many discourse genres, however—perhaps most famously in myth, as opposed to literature—statements never get attributed to an individual subject of enunciation at all. Direct discourse, in other words, is the derivative result of a deduction from or specification of un-attributed indirect discourse, when statements of collective enunciation get assigned to subjectified subjects. Collective enunciation, in any case, is the fundamental instance of language, and it always entails a specific social context.

Ultimately, the efficacy of order-words emitted by collective enunciation lies in their redundancy: "Everyone always says that..." Assent to what is supposedly the case according to an order-word depends both on the **frequency** of its repetition (the basis of signification) and on its **resonance** with who I am and the world as I imagine it to be (the basis of subjectification). And since "there is no signification independent of dominant significations, nor [any] subjectification independent of an established order of subjection," Deleuze & Guattari make pragmatics—the study of the use and effects of language in social context—the cornerstone of linguistics, rather than an ancillary or marginal sub-discipline. There can be no exclusion of factors conventionally considered to be external or extrinsic to language, because those are the factors that make language what it is and enable it to do what it does.

While their efficacy lies in their redundancy, the effects produced by order-words are what Deleuze & Guattari (following the Stoics[7]) call "incorporeal transformations." Here again, the clearest case may be a capital judicial sentence, which instantaneously transforms somebody from a defendant into a convict or a free man. This transformation is incorporeal because it has no immediate effect on the body of the accused; instead, it affects just the social standing attributed to the person, even if that will in turn have a dramatic corporeal impact on the body—liberty or death. The corporeal practices and effects take place in reciprocal presupposition with the discursive practices and vice versa, but the discursive statement itself produces only an incorporeal transformation. The same effect of incorporeal transformation characterizes speech-acts in general—they produce incorporeal transformations of the shared sense of things, the sense attributed to things by dominant significations. The slogan "the 99%" may not have produced much in the way of corporeal transformations, but it certainly produced incorporeal transformations of our shared sense of the economic and political system we inhabit. In brief, speech-acts don't establish or share or communicate a truth-relation to the world, but establish or transform the sense of what must or can be said about the world.

Making pragmatics the cornerstone of linguistics also transforms the status of constants and standardization in language. Citing the debate between Chomsky and Labov on this issue, Deleuze & Guattari side with Labov: if in a very short series of phrases a young black person passes back and forth between Black English and so-called "standard" English eighteen times, as in a case observed by Labov, the distinction between the two becomes largely beside the point: what is more important is not the constants or the standard but the variations a language undergoes in various contexts and with various speakers. Deleuze & Guattari also cite a short story by Kafka that revolves around the repetition of the performative utterance "I swear" in three very different contexts: as said by a son to his father, by a lover to his beloved, and by a witness to the judge. Despite the similarity of words, these are three completely different statements, and the aim of a pragmatic linguistics is not to extract a constant from them or reduce two of the three to mere echoes of a privileged instance (as psychoanalytic interpretations of Kafka do by privileging the Oedipal scene), but to understand all three instances on a continuum of variation so as to illuminate similarities and differences among them as expressions of different concrete assemblages.

In this light, it is no surprise that Deleuze & Guattari argue against making standard or major languages the primary object of linguistic study. "There is no [such thing as a] mother tongue [or standard language]," they insist, "only a power takeover by a dominant language" [101], and so standardizing a language so as to be able to make the linguistic study of it scientific is a preeminently **political** operation. If there are two kinds of language, they say, standard and non-standard, "high" and "low," major and minor, "the first would be defined precisely by the power (*pouvoir*) of constants, the second by the power or force (*puissance*) of variation" [101], and the field of linguistics would therefore be riven by competing attempts to confirm the power of the standard language, to affirm the validity of minor languages, and to use resources from minor languages to subvert the power and integrity of the major language—what Deleuze & Guattari call the "becoming-minoritarian" of a major language. "Minorities," they say, "are objectively definable states, states of language, ethnicity, or sex with their own ghetto territorialities, but they must also be thought of as seeds, crystals of becoming whose value is to trigger uncontrollable movements and de-territorializations of the… majority" [106]. (Consider, as a matter of style, how instructively Deleuze & Guattari use the term "crystals" here, opening a subterranean passage back to what they say about crystallization as a process of articulation and stratification, as well as forward to what they will say about the war-machine as a becomings engine operating via contagion.) I am here straying into the domains of ethics and politics, topics that are in principle reserved for later sections of this chapter, but in their treatment of linguistics, Deleuze & Guattari lay some important groundwork for what will come later (in their book as well as my exposition here). For by extracting constants from general and variegated language-usage to erect a standard or major language, linguistics ends up excluding everyone from the majority! No one conforms perfectly to the standard, and in fact everyone deviates from it to some extent—so that, paradoxically enough, becoming-minoritarian becomes the new universal: "Continuous variation constitutes the becoming-minoritarian of everybody, as opposed to the majoritarian Fact of Nobody," they say; "In erecting the figure of a universal minoritarian consciousness, one addresses powers *(puissances)* of becoming that belong to a different realm from that of Power *(Pouvoir)* and Domination," and "Becoming-minoritarian as the universal figure of consciousness is called autonomy" [106].[8]

After completing these inversions and transformations—mapping variations rather than extracting constants, elevating the minor as universal figure over the major, placing pragmatics at the heart of linguistics rather than on the margin, and so on—Deleuze & Guattari return to the concept of the order-word with which they started, and endow it with a different and additional force: not the power to impose order on people and things, but the force of dis-ordering and of transformation. There is a hidden side to order-words, in other words, which they call "passwords"—a usage of language that induces transformations, and that transforms language itself into a kind of war-machine that is better termed a metamorphosis-machine. Among other things, the invocation of such "passwords" at the end of the Linguistics plateau opens a subterranean passage directly to the Nomadology plateau, to questions of major and minor science, and to the question of the war-machine itself—all of which I will examine in the next section.

"On Several Regimes of Signs"

Right now, I turn instead to the plateau immediately following the Linguistics plateau, devoted to Several Regimes of Signs. As we saw, Deleuze & Guattari follow Hjelmslev in introducing a level of "usage" between individual speech-acts and the language-system as a whole—a level containing "collective assemblages of enunciation." But I must now add that it also contains regimes of signs, which are formations of usage on a much broader scale than collective assemblages of enunciation. Yet regimes of signs are unlike assemblages in a very important respect: assemblages are doubly-articulated, comprised of a machinic assemblage of bodies and a collective assemblage of enunciation in mutual presupposition, and therefore containing both a formalization of content and a formalization of expression (as well as substances of each). A regime of signs, by contrast, is a specific formalization of expression considered in its own right. It is true that each regime emerged or consolidated itself most fully in connection with a specific regime of power, and it is in this connection that they are most easily understood, but any given society will contain many co-existing regimes of signs, and regimes of signs can express themselves in personality-types and disorders as well as in aspects of social life. In any case, regimes of signs are not only broader in scope than assemblages, they are also more abstract. They are worthy of study because their very abstraction or autonomy from formalizations of content is what distinguishes the alloplastic mega-stratum from the other mega-strata, and what accounts for its greater speed relative to the other two. Linguistic codes are far more supple than the genetic code, and change far faster too; indeed, it is probably the case that only the sign-system of money is faster and suppler than language—but I will return to money later. Here I focus on the two regimes of signs that Deleuze & Guattari devote the most time to, although they discuss four altogether, and acknowledge that there are any number of them possible. The most important two are the signifying and the post-signifying regimes or semiotics. The other two are the pre-signifying and counter-signifying semiotics—which correspond roughly to primitive societies and the nomad war-machine, respectively, and which are usually brought in as contrast to highlight features of the first two.

The pre-signifying semiotic has the following salient contrastive features: in this semiotic, no privilege is accorded to the voice or the signifier as the sole or primary substance of expression, nor to meaning or the signified as the sole or primary form of content; here, signs are related quite directly to specific territories, rather than referring primarily to other signs, and they are not just poly-vocal but poly-semiotic, so that gesture, rhythm, dance, ritual, and so on are equally as important as vocal expression. These features contrast term by term to those with the signifying semiotic, which is characterized by "… universalizing abstraction, erection of the signifier, circularity of statements, and their correlates, the State apparatus, the instatement of the despot, the priestly caste…" [118] accompanying him, and so forth. First, let's look more closely at the signifying semiotic.

Signifying and post-signifying semiotics

The signifying semiotic first emerges in connection with despotism, and is therefore related to the conquest of one or several peoples and the de-territorialized rule from a distance of those people by the Despot and his minions. Despotism ushers in the reign of the signifier and the eclipse of reference, inasmuch as the signs emitted by the imperial Despot are no longer related directly to the territories subsisting far below his purview—and because despotic rule gets transmitted throughout his empire by a phalanx of officials or priests who interpret and spread the uniform word of the Despot to all his subjects, regardless of what languages they speak and what reference-worlds they inhabit. The signifying regime is thus inherently paranoid: not only do the conquered peoples have to constantly worry about what the decrees of the distant Despot mean, under pain of death, but as the empire expands in concentric circles from the supreme center, and circumstances become ever more varied, even the imperial priests and functionaries have cause to worry about their interpretations of the significance of what the Despot said or wrote, or what he wants—and at the same time, the Despot himself has cause to worry about being deceived, either by his minions, or by his people, or both. At the limit, the imperial decree spells a death-sentence for anyone who fails to obey or to understand its significance; "put to death or let live" is Foucault's slogan for the limit of this regime. At best, just this side of the limit, the sentence of the Despot is banishment, and the scapegoat caught defying imperial signification is not killed but sent fleeing into the desert, never to be seen by the Despot again.

The post-signifying semiotic no doubt appears more "modern" than the signifying regime—although we will see later that states today mobilize both regimes, and oscillate between a prevalence of one or the other. Where the signifying regime is characterized by paranoid-interpretive signification, the post-signifying regime is characterized by what Deleuze & Guattari call "passional subjectification." The imperial center no longer holds, the Despot turns away from his people, and so the flight into the desert no longer serves as banishment, but as a line-of-flight or escape toward autonomy, existence under reprieve. Universal deception gives way to mutual betrayal: the Despot or god has betrayed his people by turning away, and the people betray him by ignoring his decrees and fleeing in pursuit of their own subjective sovereignty. (The Protestant Reformation can serve as one illustration of this regime—but as one among many, not as a singular historical turning-point.) A new degree of subjective interiority develops, including both individualized consciousness (*cogito*) and romantic passion, with a kind of narcissistic self-righteousness informing both: "it's me—I'm special." Yet even if the Despot has turned away, he has not disappeared entirely, with the result that the regime of power becomes bureaucratic and authoritarian rather than personal and despotic, and the passion in subjectification is typically given over to grievances, whether against the authority of power or the fascination of the loved one. The transcendent centralized power of the Despot gives way to an immanent and omni-present form of power operating by normalization and the authority to define the dominant reality (which the distant Despot had neither the need nor the ability to do). Subjectified subjects now obey themselves—they obey norms they themselves have pronounced or subscribed to, instead of obeying the person of the Despot—but they end up subscribing to the norms already in effect in the dominant reality promulgated by order-words. "A new form of slavery is invented," Deleuze & Guattari conclude, "namely, being slave to oneself" [130].

It turns out, then, that despite its apparent modernity, subjectification is just as much a stratum as signification is—and as we will see in a moment, in connection with the Faciality plateau, they usually function together in a mixed semiotic where signification operates by redundancies of **frequency** in the form of what Deleuze & Guattari call a "white wall" while subjectification operates by redundancies of **resonance** in the form of a "black hole," and the two combine to form a Face. But for now I want to highlight the four major strata affecting or afflicting human beings: the organism, territorial refrains, signification-interpretation, and passional-subjectification. Compared to the relative de-territorialization of the signifying semiotic (where signs detached from reference refer only to other signs), the subjectifying semiotic involves an absolute de-territorialization tending towards autonomy (the line of flight or escape) via the development of subjective interiority. But absolute de-territorialization has dangers of its own—in this case, the possibility that subjective interiority will annihilate itself in a black hole, rather than making and sustaining contact with the plane of consistency and constructing a viable body-without-organs. "The problem, from this standpoint," as Deleuze & Guattari put it, "is to tip the most favorable assemblage from its side facing the strata to its side facing the plane of consistency" [134]—in other words, to de-stratify.

"Year Zero: faciality"

Facialization is an abstract machine in its own right, providing a specific substance of expression for the mixed regime of signification-subjectification. Only the Face as a common substance of expression assures the translatability and co-functioning of **frequency** and **resonance** as the two forms of redundancy necessary for these semiotics regimes. The concept is derived partly from empirical research in the field of psychology, partly from the visual arts (especially religious iconography), and partly from philosophy and psychoanalysis: it incorporates both the gaze from Sartre (the black hole) and the mirror-stage from Lacan (the white wall).

Although facialization is an abstract machine, it is a very specific one—not common to all of humanity (much less animals). Indeed while one of its principal results is to "remove the head from the stratum of the organism" [172] and make it function as part of the alloplastic stratum, another equally important result is to de-code the poly-vocal and poly-semiotic pre-signifying body, by over-coding the head with the Face. In this respect facialization represents an absolute de-territorialization, but one that remains negative because it sustains a regime of power by reinforcing strata—notably the strata of signification and subjectification. And it does so via two operations that Deleuze & Guattari call "bi-univocalization" and "binarization." Arborescent bi-univocalization (which was called "exclusive disjunction" in *Anti-Oedipus*) operates by converting differences into oppositions on the white wall: one is either man or woman, black or white, adult or child, rich or poor, and so on. This is how faciality reinforces the signifying semiotic in the mixed regime. Normalizing binarization operates not by the logic of either this or its opposite, but by the logic of yes or no—one either conforms to the norm or does not—and if not, it proceeds to evaluate one's degree of deviation from the norm. This is the operation that reinforces the subjectifying semiotic in the mixed regime, by consolidating subjective identities in black holes. Deleuze & Guattari draw this striking conclusion from their analysis of faciality: modern European racism does not operate by treating non-Europeans as Others and excluding them, as is often thought, but by including them and measuring their degree of deviation from European norms. Measuring non-standard deviations this way does not make racism any less abhorrent or dangerous, however: it can just as easily enable a master race to adjust its levels of tolerance of difference as justify targeting those who are different enough for annihilation [177].

The very specificity of faciality as an abstract machine, however, the fact that only "certain social formations need [the] face" [180], as Deleuze & Guattari insist, raises the question of what it is that triggers facialization in the first place. "There is a whole history behind it," they claim:

> At very different dates, there occurred a generalized collapse of all of the heterogeneous, polyvocal, primitive semiotics in favor of a semiotic of signification and subjectification. Whatever the differences between signification and subjectification, whichever prevails over the other in this case or that, whatever the varying figures assumed by their de facto mixtures—they have it in common to crush all polyvocality, set up language as a form

of exclusive expression, and operate by signifying bi-univocalization and subjective binarization. [180]

Regimes of signs are not assigned specific dates, and Deleuze & Guattari indeed insist that they do not follow a linear evolution and are always available, alone or (more often) in mixtures. And even in the "whole history behind" facialization just quoted, they claim that it can occur "at very different dates." But in the plateau's title, the faciality machine is assigned a date: Year Zero (the birth of Christ). Here is how they explain:

> If it is possible to assign the faciality machine a date—the year zero of Christ and the historical development of the White Man—it is because that is when the mixture ceased to be a splicing or an intertwining, becoming a total interpenetration in which each element suffuses the other like drops of red-black wine in white water. Our semiotic of modern White Men, the semiotic of capitalism, has attained this state of mixture in which signification and subjectification effectively interpenetrate. Thus it is in this semiotic that faciality, or the white wall/black hole system, assumes its full scope. [182]

Less surprising than the date itself—plateau-dates do after all represent the moment of highest intensity of the Event they conceptualize—is that here the faciality-machine is not associated with "very different dates," but gets specifically linked not just to the Birth of Christ, but also to the global dominance of White Men, and to the semiotic of capitalism! One way to make sense of this apparent anomaly is to suggest that the infinite debt owed to the Christian god as impossible repayment for the sacrifice of his son is transferred through Protestantism to the infinite debt owed to capital—thus forming an immense power assemblage requiring facialization to sustain itself in and through the myriad assemblages that have formed, deformed, and disappeared over the last two millennia—with no end in sight. In any case, one answer to the question of what triggers the facialization machine is clear: it is a concrete assemblage of power that triggers the abstract machine of facialization, which in turn guarantees the effective interpenetration of the signifying and subjectifying semiotics. "The face is a politics," as they say [181].

The final question Deleuze & Guattari raise concerning the faciality-machine is how to dismantle it. "If the face is a politics," they go on to say, "dismantling the face is also a politics involving real becomings, an entire becoming-clandestine" [188]. This counter-politics does not involve returning to the primitive polysemiotic head which faciality over-coded to begin with, but rather pushing faciality further, and transforming it into an exploratory "probe-head" machine. The face, they insist, is "not... a necessary stage, but... a tool for which a new use must be invented" [189]. This re-tooling is possible because any abstract machine has two fundamental states. In one state, its de-territorializations remain relative and hence consolidate strata, or become absolute but remain negative because they function in the service of a power apparatus. (This latter is the case with the faciality-machine.) In the other state, the abstract machine's de-territorializations become absolute and positive: it makes and sustains contact with the plane of consistency, becomes diagrammatic, and ultimately becomes able to transform itself into new and different machines, becoming a veritable metamorphosis-machine—a war-machine. Here, de-facialization would produce probe-head-machines to explore alternative consistencies through absolute positive de-territorialization on the plane of consistency.

In relation to the book as a whole, meanwhile, the treatment of faciality shows how image-machines can interact with regimes of signs to construct Symbolic Solutions to the human Intra-Species Social Organization Problem of different kinds, depending on the strength, degree of autonomy, and qualities (relative/absolute, negative/positive) of the de-territorializations mobilized by the abstract machines involved. What is distinctive about money as a third medium of the Symbolic order is its extreme degree of autonomy, as we will see as we turn finally to the Capture plateau.

"Apparatus of Capture" (1)

In this first approach to the Capture plateau, I will be looking only at the role of money in certain economic assemblages. There is much more to be said about apparatuses of capture, however, to which I will return in connection with the Problem of politics.

At the same time, however, examination of modes of capture will enrich our understanding of the State beyond what has already been said about the State-form of thought, inasmuch as despotism marks an important watershed among modes of capture.

The first thing to be said about economic assemblages is that they fall into two basic categories: those that involve stockpiles and those that don't. Indeed, one of the principal ways that territorial societies ward off the formation of State power and remain a-cephalous (i.e., without a head, without a head of State), as we know from the important work of French anthropologists Marcel Mauss and Pierre Clastres, is by preventing the accumulation of goods or wealth (through rituals such as *potlatch*). This type of social formation is in a sense an-economic as well as a-cephalous, in the sense that value is indistinguishable and inseparable from the codes informing everyday life and practices, and thus could just as well be called religious or social or prestige-value as "economic" value. All this changes with empire, for the Despot is in the position to—is able to and must—compare the relative value of the lands and peoples he has conquered. Paradoxically, the imperial conquest and ownership of territory actually entails a major movement of de-territorialization, in that value is now determined exogenously and from on high, by the Despot, rather than endogenously in term of the codes of local groups working the land. Despotic ownership of a stockpile of land thus becomes the basis of ground rent, which is determined by comparing the productivities of different parcels of land, and charging rent (or tribute) accordingly: only the Despot is in a position to do this.

Something very similar happens with respect to work. Just as there is no such thing as specifically "economic" value in territorial societies, there is no such thing as "work" per se, either: instead there is an indistinguishable assortment of free activities, aspects of which in connection with aspects of others "produce" enough and more than enough to sustain the group. All this changes with the conquest of people and/or the institution of slavery, whose value to the Despot is their labor-power and their labor-power alone. Or rather, their surplus-labor: the Despot has no vested interest in an amount of "necessary labor" needed to keep the laborer alive—there is always more labor-power to be had through further conquest or enslavement. So paradoxically enough, surplus-labor comes first, and at first, that was all there was. (Deleuze &

Guattari call this form of slavery "machinic enslavement" because, unlike wage-slaves who choose their employment and develop their labor-power accordingly, the subjectivity of these slaves is inconsequential: they form, and are treated as, a herd rather than a pack, so to speak.) It is important to note that this category of so-called "surplus" labor refers exclusively to the stockpile of labor employed by the Despot and his functionaries on large-scale public works projects, not the productive activity conquered peoples engaged in on their home turf.

This distinction is important because here too, something similar but if anything even more complicated transpires: those conquered peoples who were not put to forced labor on public works projects at the direct behest of the Despot were nevertheless obliged to pay tribute to him indirectly (i.e. instead of working for him directly). In a first moment of imperial de-territorialization, this means that a certain proportion of the "goods" produced by heretofore self-organized free activity is deducted from circulation within the tribe and gets redirected to the Despot. And it is the proportion of free activity responsible for that proportion of goods that becomes "work"—but here again, that portion of work is clearly **surplus** labor rather than "necessary labor." Here too, in other words, "surplus-labor" comes first, as the means of producing surplus goods to pay the Despot. But then, at a certain threshold, stockpiling surplus goods becomes less than worthless to the Despot: they spoil or rot, or prove unusable in great numbers for other reasons. This Problem ushers in a second moment of imperial de-territorialization: the payment of tribute in money form; taxation. In direct contradiction to the self-serving fictions of bourgeois economics, money in fact arose not from commercial exchange or barter, but from gift-exchange on one hand (in pre-economic territorial social formations), and from imperial taxation on the other, with the Despot having exclusive authority over the minting and circulation of currency. Because of its level of abstraction and powers of conservation, money becomes the preferred means of making the tribute collected from diverse conquered peoples calculable, comparable, more easily appropriable, and—perhaps most important—permanently accumulable. Now the imperial debt really **can** become infinite.

The empire of the Despot is thus the first great apparatus of capture or "mega-machine," and it functions in the three modes just surveyed: the Despot is simultaneously (1) the preeminent landowner who captures rent via sole ownership and comparison of land; (2) the glorious entrepreneur of large-scale projects who captures surplus-product via the ownership and/or allocation of herd-labor in machinic enslavement; and (3) the merciful conqueror who captures tribute and taxes (instead of enslaving captured peoples or putting them to death) via the ownership and circulation of money. The Despot is also the first instance (even if Jesus-Christ-capitalist is the greatest instance) of a socially functioning faciality-machine, with the white wall of the stockpile serving as a "universal" space of comparison and the Despot himself serving as the black hole of infinite accumulation.

All this changes yet again with the advent of the second great apparatus or mega-machine of capture, which is capitalism. Here, too, the same three modes are involved, but they have changed significantly. Rent now accrues to owners of capital in any form, not just to the Despot as sole landowner. Surplus is now captured predominantly in the form of surplus-value, at a substantially higher level of abstraction than surplus-product and surplus-labor, although these are still involved in the appropriation of surplus-value. Money now mediates commercial transactions more than taxation, especially in the creation of capital through financing and the appropriation of surplus-value through the wage-commodity-purchase cycle. Under capitalism, money has become crucial to all three modes of capture, and since it is purely quantitative, it is the form of expression that is most completely independent of all content-planes—even more independent than the Despotic Face, or the semiotics of language, not to mention the genetic code. But it also enables the most intensive and extensive division of labor imaginable—a division of labor which is of course simultaneously a re-articulation of labor—operating in the service of ever-increasing productive powers: intensive in the degree of specialization it fosters, and extensive in the global reach of productive activities it can coordinate. Because it is the most de-territorialized and de-territorializing element, money as capital supersedes the State as supreme engine of de-territorialization, so that the now-relative de-territorializations of the State henceforth serve as loci of re-territorialization for capital—as we will see in the Politics section.

For now, what remains is to identify the critical role of money in the specifically capitalist transformation of the faciality machine.

Yes, certainly, the Face has long since turned away—but just as certainly, it is definitely still here. Only now it is the world market made possible by money—the one truly universal element of capitalism, Deleuze & Guattari insist—that serves as the white wall of comparison, and it is transnational capital that functions as the black hole of infinite accumulation. Compared to signs and images, money fosters markets as a Solution to the human Intra-Species Social Organization Problem that operates on the highest level of abstraction, the fastest speed of transformation, and the largest scale of development—the entire globe, along with everything on it. And this makes capitalism a truly daunting—and ever shape-shifting—adversary in political struggle, as we well know...

So, to review briefly what Deleuze & Guattari's anthro-ethology contributes to their overall project, we can see that it has three overall objectives:

1) to pick up where the Refrain plateau left off, and specify how the human alloplastic mega-stratum departs from the non-human (i.e. via the Symbolic order); and

2) to develop a poststructuralist, post-humanist, and especially post-**linguistic** mapping **of** that Symbolic order—as it constitutes or proposes Solutions to the human Intra-Species Social Organization Problem; and finally

3) to analyze money as a semiotic regime operating at an even higher level of de-territorialization than language or images (via a form of expression that is now quantified), which offers human ISSO Solutions of its own, including rent, profit, the division-articulation of labor, and now worldwide markets.

To achieve these objectives, a certain number of steps are taken beyond linguistics and structuralism—and even beyond much of poststructuralism:

- linguistics is overturned in favor of regimes of signs, of which two are analyzed in some detail: the signifying regime and the subjectifying regime;

- the mixed signifying-subjectifying regime of signs is analyzed in terms of faciality, stretching all the way from Christ the Despot to contemporary capitalism;
- the role of money is specified in the development of a division-articulation of labor far beyond what was possible through refrains (although without eliminating these latter);
- a passage beyond capitalist faciality is projected in the form of a revolutionary war-machine, but a war-machine that itself faces a war-machine as adversary, in the figure of smooth capitalism.

ETHICS

The Problem: The understanding of human being outlined in the preceding sections on onto-aesthetics and anthro-ethology raises a question of ethics: how can human individuals self-organize so as to maximize their chances for productive and enjoyable de-stratification with others?

The Primary Sources: "How Do You Make Yourself a Body-Without-Organs?" is the plateau most obviously devoted to questions of ethics, but the plateaus on "One or Several Wolves" and "Three Novellas," and especially the Becomings plateau contribute significantly as well.

"One or Several Wolves"

Along with the Body-without-Organs plateau, the Wolves plateau takes a last brief look back at Freud and psychoanalysis, which had been central to the first volume of *Capitalism and Schizophrenia*. There Deleuze & Guattari showed that the Oedipus Complex does not lie at the core of the unconscious, but represents an epiphenomenon peculiar to capitalism. So here, using the case of the Wolf-Man as an example, they address the question of how to better understand the unconscious. To this end, three basic concepts are introduced: the body-without-organs (henceforth BwO), multiplicities, and the collective assemblage of enunciation.

Since the concept of the BwO was developed at length in *Anti-Oedipus* and is the focus of an entire plateau in *A Thousand Plateaus*, only its basic outlines are given here. In an important sense, the term is a misnomer, because the BwO is not so much a body deprived of organs as an assemblage of organs freed from the supposedly "natural" or "instinctual" organ-ization that makes it an organism. Whether by naturally-occurring instinct or socially-inculcated rules or habits, organs are all too often assigned particular objects and aims, when the beauty of being human (or the beauty of human being: its onto-aesthetics) is that it defies any and all pre-given forms of organization. "A body without organs is not an empty body stripped of organs," Deleuze & Guattari explain, "but a body upon which that which serves as organs (wolves, wolf eyes, wolf jaws?) is distributed according to crowd phenomena, in Brownian motion, in the form of molecular multiplicities" [30]. The BwO is thus a key element enabling the human life-form to leave both the organic mega-stratum and any established alloplastic strata behind, and to launch forth on the thread of a tune to self-organize in a multitude of different ways.

Similarly, since the concept of multiplicity was developed at length in the immediately preceding Rhizome plateau, it too receives relatively little attention here. The German mathematician Bernhard Reimann and French philosopher Henri Bergson are credited with making important distinctions between two types of multiplicity, which Deleuze & Guattari recast as a distinction between arborescent and rhizomatic multiplicities, drawing on what they had already said in the Rhizome plateau. There, the concept of multiplicity was given a botanical image: the rhizome; here it is given an ethological image: the wolf-pack; several wolves instead of the one to which Freud reduces the Wolf-Man's dream-image; a multiplicity rather than a unity of wolfing. The unconscious is a desert landscape teeming with animal populations, not a stage-set with a lone actor soliloquizing on it. And the principle of pack cohesion epitomized in wolves is Significant as a pre-human Solution to the Intra-Species Social Organization Problem that also gets adapted to address the human ISSO Problem: among humans, nomad social cohesion with be contrasted with sedentary and State-centric forms of social organization, just as pack animals can be contrasted with herd animals. Here we go, thinking with the world again. As analyzed by Swiss sociologist Elias Canetti (in *Crowds and Power*), sedentary groups or crowds are characterized by the homogeneity and divisibility of a relatively large number of members, and by a one-way leadership relation where individuals identify with the group, the group identifies with the leader, and the leader incarnates the group. Packs or bands, by contrast, are characterized by heterogeneity and role-specialization among a relatively small number of members, which endows leadership relations with some flexibility. "Canetti notes that in a pack each member is alone even in the company of others (for example, wolves on the hunt); each takes care of himself at the same time as participating in the band" [33]. Pack leaders must improvise, "play move by move," and also must "wager everything every hand," as Deleuze & Guattari put it, while the group leader "consolidates or capitalizes on past gains" [33]. At the limit, packs form multiplicities that resist totalization, unification, and reduction to a homogeneous mass, and thereby prefigure nomadism as a human Solution to the ISSO Problem.

But love, too, according to Deleuze & Guattari, is—or can be, should be—a matter of intersecting multiplicities:

> Every love is an exercise in depersonalization on a body without organs yet to be formed, and it is at the highest point of this de-personalization that someone... acquires the most intense discernibility in the instantaneous apprehension of the multiplicities belonging to him or her, and to which he or she belongs. [35]

To love somebody, they explain, involves extracting them from a mass or crowd, then finding "that person's own packs, the multiplicities he or she encloses within himself or herself," and finally merging those multiplicities with your own. Of course, here as elsewhere, Deleuze & Guattari caution that the distinction between masses and packs is an analytic one, and that in fact the two are in constant interaction in the unconscious (as well as everywhere else), with packs detaching themselves from masses, changing into or melding with other packs, only to re-integrate later into other masses, and so on.

The last major concept introduced in this early plateau is the collective assemblage of enunciation, which subsequently receives fuller treatment in the Linguistics plateau. Here directed against the notion that psychoanalysis could restore to the individual his or her "full speech," i.e., full command of what one means to say, the collective assemblage of enunciation is largely unconscious, and is composed of very diverse kinds of elements, including libidinal, social, and technical machines. There are no individual statements, Deleuze & Guattari insist, since all statements are products of machinic assemblages and therefore of collective agents of enunciation—where "collective agents" is understood to refer not just to people or societies, but to multiplicities of all kinds (which may of course include people and societies). We have seen the importance of the collective assemblage of enunciation and its relations to the machinic assemblage of bodies in Foucault's analysis of the prison-delinquency complex (in our discussion of stratification in the section on the Geology plateau). Here in the Wolves plateau, it is aimed at debunking the great ruse and delusion of psychoanalysis, namely its claim to enable individuals to finally speak in their own name, when it was actually only getting them to reproduce the statements of a specific assemblage—the psychoanalytic Oedipus Complex understood as a strictly capitalist institution trapping people in a false sense of individuality instead of freeing them to explore their multiplicities, which necessarily means exploring others' multiplicities as well.

"How do you make yourself a Body without Organs?"

This is clearly the plateau in which ethics is addressed most directly. Indeed, a kind of ethical imperative is implied in its very title: make yourself a BwO—here's how to do it. Deleuze & Guattari adopt the term from an essay by French playwright Antonin Artaud, entitled "To Have Done with the Judgment of God." In the Geology of Morals plateau, Professor Challenger describes the strata as judgments of God, and the BwO is indeed closely connected with the imperative to de-stratify. As I have already said, the term itself is not the most felicitous: "body-without-organization" would be better, to designate an inclination to dis-organ-ize the body, to de-stratify it, to free it from stratification, unification, identification and identity so as to enable experimentation with multiplicities and intensities. And it is more than an inclination: it designates an entire schizoanalytic program of depersonalization, explicitly contrasted with the program of psychoanalytic therapy:

> Where psychoanalysis says, "Stop, find your self again," we should say instead, "Let's go further still, we haven't found our BwO yet, we haven't sufficiently dismantled our self." Substitute forgetting for anamnesis, experimentation for interpretation. Find your body without organs. Find out how to make it. It's a question of life and death, youth and old age, sadness and joy. It is where everything is played out." [151]

If the BwO is where "everything is played out," that is because it is the terrain where both stratification and de-stratification vie for predominance, as we will see in a moment. But everybody has a BwO, or some BwO, to some degree at least. Anyone who has carried on a conversation beyond mere platitudes ("Nice weather we're having…") has not only set the mouth and tongue free from the "instinctual" function of ingestion by talking, but has also set the ability to make sense free from sheer habit, and constructed something of a BwO—albeit not usually a very intense one. A BwO is not a space or a place, exactly, but an occasion for experimenting with intensities, a "continually self-constructing [associated] milieu" [164, 165] on which circulate organs that have been freed from their organic functions: "'a' stomach, 'an' eye, 'a' mouth: the indefinite article… expresses the pure determination of intensity, intensive difference" [164]. Some people go to great lengths to construct maximum-intensity BwOs—masochists, for example. Their intensities are only of pain, but their BwOs are carefully constructed so as to maintain those intensities at as high a level as possible. Deleuze & Guattari cite medieval courtly love as another example of a BwO: intense affective interpersonal relationships are maintained by an entire cultural program designed to prevent the consummation of desire. For ironically enough, orgasmic pleasure is one of the major obstacles to maintaining high-intensity desire, inasmuch as orgasm brings desire to an end, or at least diminishes its intensity considerably. The other major obstacles to understanding the BwO are to construe desire in terms of either lack or some transcendent ideal of impossibility, as if the intensity of courtly love were caused by something that's missing, or by some kind of other-worldly devotion, when it is a very practical matter of constituting a BwO in order to sustain desire at maximum intensity:

> It would be an error to interpret courtly love in terms of a law of lack or an ideal of transcendence. The renunciation of external pleasure, or its delay, its infinite regress, testifies on the contrary to an achieved state in which desire no longer lacks anything but fills itself and constructs its own field of immanence. Pleasure [unlike desire] is an affection of a person or a subject; it is the only way for persons to "find themselves" in the process of desire that exceeds them; pleasures, even the most artificial, are re-territorializations. But the question is precisely whether it is necessary to find oneself [to which the answer is no]. Courtly love does not love the self, any more than it loves the whole universe in a celestial or religious way. It is a question of making a body without organs upon which intensities pass... not in the name of a higher level of generality or a broader extension, but by virtue of singularities that can no longer be said to be personal and intensities that can no longer be said to be extensive. [156]

Much the same is true in masochism (as Deleuze showed in his early study of Sacher-Masoch himself, *Coldness and Cruelty*): it would be an error to imagine that pain is endured merely in order to achieve pleasure, when in fact pain is used to sever the "instinctive" connection between desire and the extrinsic pleasure of orgasm, so as to prevent the latter from interrupting the former, the "continuous process of positive desire" [155]. The BwO, in other words, is where or when desire "constructs its own field of immanence" and thereby maximizes its potential, a kind of schizoanalytic version of the Freudian notion of "polymorphous perversity"—except that the BwO is not a premature stage of sexuality to be abandoned for the sake of "mature" hetero-reproductive sex, but an always-potentially-present state of desire to be recovered from the stultifying habits and compulsory norms afflicting behaviors of all kinds. Like the plane of consistency itself, then, BwOs are subject to stratification of various kinds, both organic ("instincts," the organism) and alloplastic (cultural and institutional norms, neurotic habits, and so on). They are the locus of an on-going struggle between stratification and de-stratification, between normalization and free experimentation, autonomy.

The ethical question thus becomes, how can we make good on the potential of BwOs, how can we de-stratify? How do we free ourselves from the stratum of the organism, from the stratum of signification and interpretation and from the stratum of subjectification and subjection? The answer, in a word, is: cautiously. The point of departure is a BwO that oscillates continually

> between the surfaces that stratify it and the plane [of consistency] that sets it free. If you free it with too violent an action, if you blow apart the strata without taking precautions, then instead of drawing the plane you will be killed, plunged into a black hole, or even dragged toward catastrophe. Staying stratified—organized, signified, subjected—is not the worst that can happen: the worst that can happen is if you throw the strata into demented or suicidal collapse, which brings them back down on us heavier than ever. This is how it should be done: Lodge yourself on a stratum, experiment with the opportunities it offers, find an advantageous place on it, find potential movements of de-territorialization, possible lines of flight, experience them, produce flow conjunctions here and there, try out continuums of intensities segment by segment, have a small plot of new land at all times. It is through a meticulous relation with the strata that one succeeds in freeing lines of flight, causing conjugated flows to pass and escape and bringing forth continuous intensities for a BwO. [...]
>
> And how necessary caution is, the art of dosages, since overdose is a danger. You don't do it with a sledgehammer, you use a very fine file. You invent self-destructions that have nothing to do with the death drive. Dismantling the [organism] has never meant killing yourself, but rather opening the body to connections that presuppose an entire assemblage, circuits, conjunctions, levels and thresholds, passages and distributions of intensity, and territories and de-territorializations measured with the craft of a surveyor. [160]

A strong dose of caution is necessary because of the dangers Deleuze & Guattari now recognize as inherent to BwOs (quite unlike their unbridled enthusiasm for them in *Anti-Oedipus*).

While careful and productive de-stratification is the ethical ideal, there is a danger of de-stratifying too rapidly or wildly—the danger of over-dosing, in both the literal sense (over-dosing on drugs) and the figurative sense (over-dosing on too much de-stratification). But there are also BwOs belonging to the strata themselves, BwOs that proliferate uncontrollably and end up being destructive, such as cancer, inflation, and fascism. The ethical challenge for desire, Deleuze & Guattari conclude, is "distinguishing between that which pertains to stratic proliferation [cancerous BwOs], or else too-violent de-stratification [over-dosing], and that which pertains to the construction of the plane of consistency" [165] where your BwO can intersect or merge productively with those of others, as you launch forth on the thread of a tune to improvise with the world.

"Three Novellas, or 'what happened?'"

The Novellas plateau starts with a surprising excursus into literary genre theory, defining the novella genre in terms of the question "what happened?" in contrast with the tale, which asks and answers the question "what will happen?" The question is germane to the issue of ethics because it seeks to uncover incorporeal transformations that were imperceptible when they first occurred, but may become visible by careful reading of what one might call the life-lines of those affected by the repercussions of those transformations. "For we are made of lines," Deleuze & Guattari suggest, "… life lines, lines of luck and misfortune…" [194], and so on. What could have happened, what must have happened for the course of this life to have been transformed in these ways? Through brief analyses of three novellas by Henry James, F. Scott Fitzgerald, and Pierrette Fleutiaux, they show how the struggle between stratification and de-stratification on BwOs can be translated into a problematic of lines, thereby forging a connection between the earlier BwO plateau and the immediately following Micropolitics and Segmentarity plateau, which as we shall see in the next section is also devoted to lines, but in a more political than ethical frame. Here, lines serve to diagnose or understand lives, whether those of novella characters, literary authors, or ordinary mortals.

Our lives are composed of three basic types of lines, Deleuze & Guattari conclude from their readings of the three novellas: "a line of rigid and clear-cut segmentarity; a [supple] line of molecular segmentarity; and an abstract line, a line of flight" [197]. The rigidly-segmented line delineates the major components of our lives: where we work, and in what capacity (professions and trades, with their special refrains); where we live, and with whom: whether we are man or woman, married or single, adult or child, and so forth. Along this line, the breaks between segments marking major life-transformations are perfectly clear-cut: leaving home for the first time, marrying or divorcing, accepting a new job, and so on. But beneath this rigid line of clearly-demarcated segments lies another line, a supple line of molecular segmentarity, where imperceptible micro-transformations are constantly occurring, moving in all directions, some of which sometimes contribute to a major life-transformation: that's when we ask what could have happened, without our noticing, on the line of molecular segmentarity to produce such a momentous transformation? (Kafka is one of the great cartographers of rigid and supple lines, as Deleuze & Guattari show in their book on him; they also cite another literary author, Nathalie Sarraute, for the diagnoses her works provide of the ways supple lines of micrological "subconversation" co-exist with and subtend the macrological conversations characters carry on with one another [196–7].) Then there is the third kind of line, lines of flight or absolute rupture, which sail past the point of no return, change everything, transform lives so completely as to make them unrecognizable: "One has become imperceptible and clandestine in motionless voyage. Nothing can happen, can have happened, any longer" [199]. And of course the three kinds of line always operate in mixtures and in relation to one another. So just as the BwO ended up embodying a crucial ambiguity between the forces of stratification and de-stratification, the same is true of the co-existence of lines: "supple segmentarity is caught between the two other lines, ready to tip to one side or the other; such is it ambiguity" [205].

This co-existence, finally, does not obviate the need to identify the dangers inherent in each line. Obviously, conformity and stagnation are the problem with the line of rigid segmentarity. But supple segmentarity risks recreating on its own line some of the same problems encountered on the rigid line, among which

Deleuze & Guattari mention "micro-Oedipuses, microformations of power, [and] microfascisms" [205]. The line of absolute rupture, meanwhile, risks overdosing and spinning into a void—and indeed Deleuze & Guattari wonder aloud why in so many literary works this most promising of lines gets "imbued with such singular despair in spite of its message of joy" [205]. For in principle, the line of flight involves a movement of absolute de-territorialization that could ideally make everybody become-everything, or create a becoming-everything of/for everybody (*faire de tout-le-monde un devenir* [F244]) [E200]. It may be, however, that the note of despair Deleuze & Guattari detect in so many great authors arises from an incompatibility or incommensurability between the scope of the ambition to create such a becoming-everything of everybody and the scope that a focus on individual lives, works of literature, or ethics allows. This notion of incommensurability is certainly not something Deleuze & Guattari themselves would be satisfied with: the schizoanalytic approach to the three lines that compose us, they insist, is "immediately practical and political," and "the lines it brings [to our attention] could equally be the lines of a life, a work of literature or art, or a society, depending on which system of coordinates is chosen" [203–4]. In any case, I return to the becoming-everything of everybody in connection with the system of coordinates of politics in the next section. But in preparation, I turn now to the Becomings plateau to further explore the concept of becoming itself.

"Becoming-intense, Becoming-animal, Becoming-imperceptible..."

The Becomings plateau is the longest one in the book (slightly longer than the Nomadology plateau), and like the Geology plateau, it is staged or framed—this time as a series of what appear to be recollections on the part of a "moviegoer," a "naturalist," a "Bergsonian," a "Sorcerer," and so forth. Indeed, the first recollection, "Memories of a Moviegoer," begins with the words "I recall the fine film *Willard*" [233], which appear to anchor the memory in a specific subject (is it Deleuze? Guattari? an anonymous fictional character?—we are never told). But then, after announcing that he/they/whoever "will recount the story in broad outline," this subject-narrator admits to being unreliable ("My memory of it is not necessarily accurate" [233])—thus ending up in a position of authority as questionable as that of Professor Challenger in the Geology plateau. And the authority in question hardly becomes more reliable when the narrative voice self-identifies as "We sorcerers" [239] and addresses us as "fellow sorcerers" [241] later in this plateau. Moreover, as the series of memories unfolds, the sense of the preposition "of" in the series' sub-titles becomes increasingly ambiguous: the first section, "Memories of a Moviegoer," seems to refer unequivocally to the subject of memory, someone who recalls seeing a film; in later sections such as "Memories of a Haecceity" and "Memories of a Molecule," however, it seems as though "Haecceity" and "Molecule" are objects rather than subjects of recollection; they appear to designate what is being recalled rather than the agent doing the recalling. But if the earth can think (as per the title of the Geology plateau), why can't molecules remember? This confusion (no doubt intentional) between subjects and objects of recollection is affirmed and compounded late in the plateau, when they distinguish categorically between becomings (the very topic of the plateau) and memories, even going so far as to say that "Becoming is an anti-memory"!—at which point they abruptly change their minds and declare retroactively that "Wherever we used the word 'memories' in the preceding pages, we were wrong to do so; we meant to say 'becoming,' we were saying becoming" [294]. (Does this correspond to the transmutation of the linear past into the realm of the virtual?) "Have short-term ideas" is what they recommended at the end of the introductory Rhizome plateau [25]: is that why the longest plateau is divided into a series of short sections? But then what does it mean when 15 pages from the end of the plateau, they ask us to mentally retrace our steps and replace "memories" with "becomings" across the preceding 60 pages? Long-term memory is a rigid line anchored in a subject and a specific point in the past; short-term memory is rhizomatic: what light does this cast on the opening of the plateau: "I recall..."? Does the rhythm of the plateau as a whole express the ambiguity of the supple line, oscillating between tree and rhizome, between long-term and short-term memory, between memory and becoming, between stratification and de-stratification? And, most important, why is becoming defined as an anti-memory in the first place?

Various lines of becoming

Schizoanalysis had already recommended replacing the psychoanalytic program of remembering and interpreting the past (a program of anamnesis) with a program focused on improvising and improving the future. "Substitute forgetting for anamnesis" was its slogan: "[substitute] experimentation for interpretation. Find your body without organs" [151]. The BwO is where or when becomings take place, becomings that draw lines-of-flight away from rigid segmentarity in the direction of the plane of consistency of desire. One way to pose the question of ethics, then, is: how can we draw such lines? Here is the map that Deleuze & Guattari propose: As a feature of arborescence, long-term memory draws a line between two points in time: a point in the present and a point in the past. In a similar way, phantasy draws a line between two contiguous points in the unconscious. A line of becoming, by contrast—like an arrow in flight once it is freed both from its point of origin in the archer's intentions and its point of impact in the once-intended target—

> ...is not defined by points that it connects.... On the contrary, it passes *between* points, it comes up through the middle, it runs perpendicular to the points first perceived, transversally to the localizable relation to distant or contiguous points. A point is always a point of origin. But a line of becoming has neither beginning nor end, departure nor arrival, origin nor destination.... A line of becoming has only a middle. [293]

A line of becoming has only a middle, *un milieu*, and it arises only *au milieu*, in-between the points that it leaves behind. Rather than a relation of opposition—subject/object—or a relation of imitation—subject/subject—becomings involve an asymmetrical alliance between a **subject** and a **medium** of becoming. The line of becoming does not connect one to the other, nor does it originate in one or the other: it arises between the two and leaves them both behind. It is not an imitation, but the actualization of an already-existing virtual potential in the subject of the becoming provoked contagiously by a molecular element in the medium of the becoming. Thus in the famous example of the becoming-woman of man, a man as subject of the becoming is withdrawn from the majority, while a feature of woman as medium of the becoming gets detached from the minority. Clearly the man does not simply become "a" woman; nor does he imitate "the" woman as molar entity: rather, the man becomes something-other-than majoritarian-male by virtue of integrating an element drawn from the woman as minority. In a similar vein, becoming-animal does not involve "a resemblance or analogy to the animal… [but rather] the production of the molecular animal (whereas the 'real' animal is trapped in its molar form and subjectivity)" [275]. "There is no subject of the becoming except as a de-territorialized variable of the majority," Deleuze & Guattari explain, and "there is no medium of becoming except as a de-territorialized variable of a minority" [292]. In the case of becoming-woman, it is clear that elements from the complete repertoire of molecular behaviors and affects common to the human life-form, which get rigidly divided and distributed over the two sexes to **make** the two of them into a molar binary opposition, can be re-distributed in the course of becomings-woman. The double-becoming of wasp and orchid is in some respects far more striking: they don't share genetic material, but each has nonetheless become the subject of a becoming-the-other by capturing an element of its behavioral or morphological repertoire, each serving as medium for the other's becoming. The becoming-animal between humans and wolves, to take another instance, lies somewhere in-between: regardless of how much genetic material or mammalian "instinct" we may share, there are elements of behavior and social structure that pass between us and them—including role-specialization and pack behaviors as Solutions to the Intra-Species Social Organization Problem.

Becomings-animal are indeed where the plateau begins, before moving on to discuss becoming-woman, becoming-imperceptible, and finally everybody-becoming-everything. Echoing the Wolves plateau and the Rhizome plateau, becomings-animal are associated exclusively with pack animals. It may be that there are no becomings-cattle for the same reasons (which I will examine shortly) that there are no becomings-man; it may be that herd behavior is already implied in the State-form of Intra-Species Social Organization. In any case, Deleuze & Guattari are adamant: "We do not become-animal without a fascination for the pack, for multiplicity" [239–40]. But it is not a question of which animals are pack animals "by nature" and which aren't: a lone animal may express the appeal of pack multiplicity that attracts human becomings-animal in the first place, by serving as their medium. "Every animal is fundamentally a... pack," Deleuze & Guattari insist [239]. And if becomings-animal exert a fascination over us, it is because pack-multiplicities always operate via contagion rather than filiation. Whereas families, species, and States always, to the greatest extent of which they are capable, internalize the linear or lineal process of their own perpetuation, becomings, by contrast, operate laterally, and must always start over anew. Orchid and wasp are each crucial to the other's survival, but there is no orchid-wasp hybrid. Pack-multiplicities "form, develop, and are transformed by contagion" [242], Deleuze & Guattari insist, and it is this feature that makes them a key medium for becomings-animal. So all becomings—becomings-animal, becomings-woman, and so on—involve multiplicities, and in fact, multiplicities are themselves always defined in terms of their becomings or lines-of-flight, by that part of the border of a multiplicity that will open to another multiplicity in a double-becoming, or that will bud and thus transform the multiplicity itself by adding another patch or dimension to it. Deleuze & Guattari call the segments of a multiplicity's borderline that are most susceptible to becomings the "anomalous," and it is these anomalous zones that harbor the greatest potential for change.

If a multiplicity develops a more or less continuous and consistent rhythm of change, repeated buddings in the same direction or of a similar tendency or orientation produce a line-of-flight, forming what Deleuze & Guattari instructively call a **fiber**, "a string of borderlines, a continuous line of borderlines (fiber) following which the multiplicity changes" [249]. These fibers of becoming can in turn, under propitious conditions, intersect and overlap and intertwine with other becoming fibers, and in the process they draw a plane of consistency that has precisely the rhizomatic consistency of felt, and of jazz improvisation. Earlier, I defined the plane of consistency as the aggregate of all virtual potential, but it could equally well be described as the aggregate or patchwork of all possible fibers of becoming, of all possible lines of flight. The ethical imperative is to open ourselves up to experimentation with such lines of becoming, to leave home on the thread of a tune in order to improvise with the world and form meshwork with it.

Following Spinoza, Deleuze & Guattari assess the potentials for and results of ethical experimentation in terms of affects, the forces a body harbors to act and to be affected by other bodies and actions. Speaking from their ethical perspective (which they share with German ethologist von Uexküll), Deleuze & Guattari explain that "a racehorse is more different from a workhorse than a workhorse is from an ox" [257], because the workhorse and ox share certain capacities for action and being acted on that are not shared with the racehorse. Even more important, bodies are defined in terms of their capacities to interact with other bodies:

> We know nothing about a body until we know what it can do, in other words, what its affects are, how they can or cannot enter into composition with other affects, with the affects of another body, either to destroy that body or to be destroyed by it, either to exchange actions and passions with it or to join with it in composing a more powerful body. [257]

So experimentation with the anomalous borderline of becomings entails determining whether adding a specific dimension to our current assemblage—that is to say, entering into a specific becoming or into a double-becoming with another assemblage—will augment our power to act and/or enjoy being affected by other assemblages or not. If it does, the experiment will have been an ethical success. If not, we stop and go experiment elsewhere and otherwise.

All becomings are molecular, in the sense that a molecular element gets detached from a majoritarian molar subject by virtue of its indiscernibility from a molecular element arising contagiously from the medium of a minority subject. But given that—relative to a certain humanist-androcentric perspective attributable to the standard adult White Man—animals, women and girls are considered "lower" forms of life, becomings-animal, becomings-woman, and becomings-girl take pride of place among the plethora of potential becomings. Becoming is always a movement away from the molar toward the molecular, away from the majority toward the minority, away from the oppressor and toward the oppressed. So if "all becomings begin with and pass through becoming-woman" [277], it is first and foremost because Man occupies the supreme position of power (*pouvoir*) and represents the standard norm against which differences are measured.

Why are there so many becomings of man, but no becoming-man? First because man is majoritarian par excellence, whereas becomings are minoritarian; all becoming is a becoming-minoritarian. When we say majority, we are referring not to a greater relative quantity but to the determination of a state or standard in relation to which larger quantities, as well as the smallest, can be said to be minoritarian: white-man, adult-male, etc. Majority implies a state of domination, not the reverse.... It is perhaps the special situation of women in relation to the man-standard that accounts for the fact that becomings, being minoritarian, always pass through a becoming-woman. [291]

And if becoming-girl plays almost as important a role as becoming-woman, it is largely because of the ethical imperative that adults engage in becomings-child, inasmuch as being adult is part of the standard norm. Here again we encounter the categorical difference between memory and becoming, for becoming-child does not mean regressing to one's childhood at all—even as a stage in therapy. Becoming-child has nothing to do with memory, conscious or unconscious. ("This will be a childhood," Virginia Woolf writes, "but it must not be my childhood" [294].) Becoming-child is more like becoming-wolf-cub: it means accessing or retrieving a behavioral repertoire most of which has been selected out or repressed in the process of reaching mature (molar) adulthood. It means restoring a kind of "polymorphous perversity," if you will, provided we understand this as a repertoire of means of enjoyment that bear no necessary relation to reproduction or even to "sexuality." It is in this sense that Deleuze & Guattari insist that "the child does not **become** an adult any more than the girl **becomes** a woman; the girl is the becoming-woman of each sex, just as the child is the becoming-young of every age" [277]. Of course, girls grow up to be women, but this is not a becoming: ordinarily, this is a process whereby their molecular multiplicity gives way to molar maturity, especially as certain of their bodily capacities (affects) are captured and placed in the service of hetero-normative reproduction—the capacities of "the body they *steal* from us in order to fabricate opposable organisms" [276]. If "even" women should engage in becomings-woman and becomings-girl, then, it is as molar women that they do so, in order to escape molar adulthood and womanhood and regain access to their molecularity, almost as much as men need to engage in becomings-woman to escape their molar positions and regain their molecularity.

Another reason becomings-woman are so important (for everyone, but especially men) is because ethics is ultimately a matter of desire rather than obedience, of what you want to do rather than what you must do—or as Spinoza might put it, of what you **would** really want to do, if you fully understood the causes and consequences of doing so and not doing so. Becomings-woman are important inasmuch as they free us from the molar-binary organization of the sexes (which is hardly improved, Deleuze & Guattari add, by "a bisexual organization within each sex" [278]). Sexuality is instead a question of multiplicities and becomings:

> Sexuality brings into play too great a diversity of conjugated becomings [to be accounted for adequately by either the binary organization of the sexes or a bisexual organization within each sex]; these [becomings] are like *n* sexes, an entire war-machine through which love passes.... Sexuality is the production of a thousand sexes, which are so many uncontrollable becomings. [278-9]

Sexual becomings thus always take place "in-between" (*au milieu*), in a process of double-becoming that de-personalizes each of the partners at the same time that it gives each of them access to their potential molecular multiplicity in and through the other (as simultaneously subject and medium of becoming). And if becomings-woman assume primary importance, it is once again in order to release molecular lines from their capture in rigid molar segmentarity—and in this respect, "the woman as a molar entity *has to become-woman*" [275] and thereby produce a molecular woman **just as much** for her own sake as for the becomings-woman of the man.

Crucially, this does **not** mean that women simply abandon their molar position altogether. Deleuze & Guattari are clear that it is "indispensable for women to conduct a molar politics, with a view to winning back their own organism, their own history, their own subjectivity" [276]. But at the same time, they say, it is "necessary to conceive of a molecular women's politics that slips into molar confrontations, and passes under or through them" [276]. (Here again, we are reminded of Kafka as the great cartographer of the rhizome of molecular politics operating beneath the apparent organizational chart of macropolitical power.) Much the same can be said about the prospects for minorities and the concept of becoming-minoritarian. Even though minorities such as blacks are clearly "in the minority," there is still a critical difference between becoming-minoritarian and being-in-a-minority or being-a-minority. If "even women should become-woman," then "even blacks, as the Black Panthers said, should become-black" [291; translation modified]. In one case there is a re-territorialization on the molar status of being-(in)-a-minority, and in the other, there is a molecular transformation affecting both the majority and the minority, hopefully with positive effects for all concerned. This is not to say that anyone should abandon the pursuit of full rights for minorities, any more than for women—on the contrary—but rather to suggest that there is always a molecular becoming-minoritarian accompanying or underlying it. I will return to this duality in connection with politics in the next section.

Becoming-imperceptible and haecceities

But at this point, I need to consider the relations among the different kinds of becomings I have discussed so far. For at the limit of a series of becomings of increasing intensity—becomings-woman, becomings-girl, becomings-animal, becomings-molecular—lies the ultimate becoming: becoming-imperceptible. "A kind of order or apparent progression can be established for the segments of becoming in which we find ourselves," Deleuze & Guattari say: "becoming-woman, becoming-child; becoming-animal, -vegetable, or -mineral; becomings-molecular of all kinds, becomings-particle" [272]. And "what are they all rushing toward?" Deleuze & Guattari ask: "without a doubt, toward a becoming-imperceptible. The imperceptible is the immanent end of becoming, its cosmic formula" [279]. As we have already seen, lines of becoming, lines-of-flight, the tendency of BwOs to de-stratify—all lead away from the plane of organization and toward the plane of consistency. This movement of de-territorialization is immanent to the chaosmos as a difference-engine (although chaosmosis also entails, of course, an accompanying moment of re-territorialization, consolidation, and stratification, too). The plane of organization contains all the strata and mega-strata, including—once we reach the organic and alloplastic mega-strata—the organization of organisms, of signification, and of subjectification. Lines-of-flight and becomings tip these strata away from the plane of organization, detach molar beings from this plane and lead them in the direction of "the (anorganic) imperceptible, the (asignifying) indiscernible, and the (asubjective) impersonal" [279]. This is one dimension of the plane of consistency, the sense in which it is populated, as I have said, by all the virtual potential, all the potential becomings that comprise the chaosmos, by all that the consistency of **this** chaosmos (with its "constants") could ever enable. But at the same time—or rather, in a completely different time, the time that Deleuze & Guattari call the time of "Aeon" (as opposed to "Chronos" or chronological time)—the plane of consistency is populated immanently by "haecceities." *Haecceities* constitute the absolute degree-zero of related difference: this and that and this and...; this with that with this with.... Each *haecceity* designates a pure "this-here-now." They are therefore impossible to define, and can only be described by example:

> There is a mode of individuation very different from that of a person, subject, thing, or substance. We reserve the name *haecceity* for it. A season, a winter, a summer, an hour, a date... [each has] a perfect individuality lacking nothing, even though this individuality is different from that of a thing or a subject.... In Charlotte Brontë, everything is in terms of wind, things, people, faces, loves, words. Lorca's "five in the evening," when love falls and fascism rises. That awful five in the evening! We say, "What a story!" "What heat!" "What a life!" to designate a very singular individuation. The hours of the day in Lawrence, in Faulkner. [261]

While the plane of organization is populated by (among other things) forms and subjects, this dimension of the plane of consistency consists only of *haecceities* composed of elements or particles, speeds and affects. Indeed, while one dimension of the plane of consistency is drawn by the ethical and political lines-of-flight and becomings that tend in its direction, this other dimension gets mapped purely in terms of longitudes and latitudes: the elements of which bodies are composed along with their relative speeds (longitude), and their capacities to act and be acted upon, to affect and be affected (latitude). If becoming-molecular leads us to a becoming-imperceptible, then, it is because beneath or beyond or at/as the "immanent end" of all becomings-molecular lies the cosmic and the particulate—a chaosmos composed of particles before they acquire forms and functions, movements at speed before they attain velocity and direction. At the limit, *haecceities* as this dimension of the plane of consistency constitute the **medium** of all molecular becomings, while the **subjects** of all becomings emerge by disengaging from molar being and strata on the plane of organization.

While *haecceities* comprise the form of content of the plane of consistency, it also has a corresponding form of expression: "*Indefinite article + proper name + infinitive verb* constitutes the basic chain of expression, correlative to the least formalized contents, from the standpoint of a semiotic that has freed itself from both formal significations and personal subjectifications" [263]. Proper names designate not individual subjects, but events (as in hurricanes or military campaigns); moreover, "the proper name is not the subject of a tense but the agent of an infinitive" [264]. Infinitive verbs designate potential acts or occurrences in the smooth or non-pulsed, non-metrical time of *Aeon*, without attributing them to (grammatical or individual) subjects or situating them in the linear timeframe of *Chronos*. The use of indefinite pronouns and articles, finally, detaches agency from a specific subject and relocates it in a collective assemblage of enunciation (in which "one" can pronounce death sentences, to take an example from the prison-delinquency complex again), and distributes being over a non-specific and unquantifiable set of entities ("a" prison, "some" prisoners). The expression of *Aeonic* events can therefore take forms like "wasp to meet orchid" [265] or "some people to occupy," which maximize the potential of a given *haecceity* to serve as a medium of becoming. "The contents of [such] chains of expression... are those that can be assembled for a maximum number of occurrences and becomings" [265].

The question then becomes how the pure immanence of *haecceities* on this dimension of the plane of consistency furthers the ultimate tendency of all becomings, which is becoming-imperceptible. Here again, comparison with the plane of organization is helpful. For this plane always adds itself as an extra dimension (n + 1) to the forms and subjects it organizes: they are what appears as molar entities, while the plane itself does not, as that which determines them as molar beings. On the plane of consistency, by contrast, there is no formal organization separate from the particles themselves, no velocity or direction separate from their relative speeds, no specific function separate from their capacities, no subjective desire separate from their perceptions: in this case, "the plane itself is perceived at the same time that it allows us to perceive the imperceptible" [267]; we have reached "a perception of things, thoughts, desires in which desire, thought, and the thing have invaded all of perception: the imperceptible finally perceived... the moment when desire and perception meld" [283], when desire is no longer lacking anything and has become indistinguishable from what it desires, from what incites desire. Things, thoughts and desires must become indistinguishable and unrecognizable, in other words, as the necessary condition for their being perceived as components of a *haecceity*: a perception of some "this-here-now" rather than of *b*-as-an-instance-of-a-category-*B*, occurring at moment *t* on timeline *t-t'*, and taking place at point *x, y, z* in striated Cartesian-coordinate space. And in this light, becoming-imperceptible as the limit and immanent end of all becomings appears as a precise correlate of nomad thought, the limit and ultimate tendency of all philosophy: for just as the pure immanence of nomad thought is achieved by eliminating all images of thought standing between it and the outside, when its speed and orientation precisely correlate with the speed and orientation of the outside, becoming-imperceptible is achieved by eliminating all forms of organization, signification, and subjectification standing between our desires and our perceptions so that they correlate precisely, thus enabling us to launch forth from home on the thread of a tune, to improvise with the World, and ultimately to meld with it.

Becoming-imperceptible as the immanent end of all becomings is thus crucial to the impossible-to-translate but all-important "everybody-becoming-everything" or "the minoritarian becoming-everything of everybody" (*devenir-tout-le-monde*). Every becoming taken to the limit dissolves its subject (the subject-of-becoming) in some *haecceity* as medium-of-becoming, thereby rendering it imperceptible and indiscernible from the world of all *haecceities*:

> It is in this sense that everybody-becoming-everything [*devenir-tout-le-monde*], making the world a becoming, is to world, to make a world or worlds, in other words, to find one's proximities and zones of indiscernibility.... Imperceptibility, indiscernibility, and impersonality — the three virtues. To reduce oneself to an abstract line, a trait, in order to find one's zone of indiscernibility with other traits and in this way enter... haecceity.... One is then like grass: one has made the world, everybody/everything, into a becoming... because one has suppressed in oneself everything that prevents us from slipping between things and growing in the midst of things. One has combined "everything" (*le "tout"*): the indefinite article, the infinitive-becoming, and the proper name.... [280, translation modified]

All becomings, as we have seen, tip or tend toward the plane of consistency. And the absolute limit of becoming as becoming-imperceptible, I can now say, is the dimension of the plane of consistency composed of *haecceities*: pure immanence and the becoming-everything of everybody. At this limit, ethics merges with and ultimately dissolves into aesthetics, in the pure de-personalized enjoyment of some "this-here-now" or other. Ethical experimentation, then, takes place between the strata that we are always leaving on the thread of a tune, but that we nevertheless always necessarily inhabit, and this everybody-becoming-everybody as the limit of all becomings. The political implications of the all-important "minoritarian becoming-everything of everybody" are, however, another matter—and I turn to them in the next section. But the principal ethical criterion remains the one that Deleuze & Guattari develop from Spinoza and Nietzsche: it is always a question of whether a given becoming augments our ability to act and our mutual enjoyment of affecting and being affected by others. So go ahead: become-woman, man! And become-everything, everybody!

POLITICS

The Problem: Deleuze & Guattari often described *A Thousand Plateaus* as a book of political philosophy, and it is a topic I have touched on frequently in the preceding sections, as philosophical interventions were made in a variety of other fields with the ultimate aim of making the outside world more susceptible to beneficial transformation. This chapter addresses politics directly, posing the question of how the human life-form can be understood to self-organize socially in ways that account for herd as well as pack behaviors, for repressive despotic tyranny as well as expansive economic imperialism, for the constraints of rigid stratification as well as the flights of de-stratification that can change social life for the better.

The Primary Sources: The plateau of most immediate relevance is obviously "Micropolitics and Segmentarity," but the Nomadology and Capture plateaus are also important for mapping the terrain of political struggles, targeting major adversaries, and surveying available resources.

"Micropolitics and segmentarity"

The Micropolitics plateau begins with a strong intervention in the field of political anthropology, and ends up establishing a typology of "lines" that will be important for both politics and ethics (notably in the Novellas plateau). Political anthropology is structured by a basic dichotomy between what it calls "segmentary" or State-less (a-cephalous) societies and political or State-centric societies. Deleuze & Guattari reject this dichotomy: all societies are segmented in one way or another. The important distinction lies instead between two different forms of segmentarity: supple and rigid. Primitive territorial societies exhibit supple or molecular segmentarity, which is "characterized by a polyvocal *code* based on lineages and their varying situations and relations, and an itinerant *territoriality* based on local, overlapping divisions. Codes and territories, clan lineages and tribal territorialities, form a fabric of relatively supple segmentarity" [209]. Furthermore, within primitive societies it is "the distinction between these two elements, the tribal system of territories and the clan system of lineages, that prevents resonance [among rigid segments]" [212], which is typical of State-centric societies. But then Deleuze & Guattari add something completely new: each mode of segmentarity can take three different forms: binary, circular, and linear.

Segmentarities

We are already familiar with the State mode of binary segmentation from our examination of the faciality machine. State or molar segmentation is inherently dualistic, operating as we saw via bi-univocalization (man vs. woman, rich vs. poor) and binarization (white or not, and if not what complexion; adult or not, and if not what age; etc.). Primitive segmentation, by contrast, produces dualisms as a by-product of larger operations—as when a matrimonial pairing (man/woman) results from a complex of exchanges involving at least three clans within a tribe [210]. In a similar vein, circular segmentarity in primitive societies involves domains with different centers: for example, the exchange of goods, the exchange of information, the exchange of women, and the exchange of myths will each take place within its own segment of social life, and while there may be considerable overlap among the segments, each retains an important degree of autonomy from the others: their centers remain distinct from one another. (Thus Lévi-Strauss characterizes the role of the shaman in such societies as performing temporary translations or negotiations between different segments that never align with one another on a permanent basis.) To put the distinction another way, primitive segmentarity is animistic or polytheistic in form, while State segmentarity is monotheistic. That does not mean that State societies are any less segmented: they, too, have distinct domains, but now the circles are concentric, and their centers resonate in a single center, the central black hole of the Despotic Face:

> The central State is constituted not by the abolition of circular segmentarity but by a concentricity of distinct circles, or the organization of a resonance among centers. *There are already just as many power centers in primitive societies; or, if one prefers, there are still just as many in State societies.* The latter, however, behave as apparatuses of resonance; they organize resonance, whereas the former inhibit it. [211]

The State-form of linear segmentarity, finally, results from the overcoding and striation of space ("a substitution of space for places and territories" [212]), in which each segmentation is homogenized according to its own standard of measure, while at the same time becoming susceptible to comparison with and translation into all the other measured segments (which as we saw takes place on the white wall of the head-of-State's Face). Rigid segments are controlled from a measuring center that lines up with the other segment-centers, whereas supple line-segments bifurcate freely, and bud and develop in new directions from either end without being subordinate to a center.

We have already seen an example of supple line-segmentation, when an open multiplicity's repeated buddings in the same direction produce a line-of-flight and form a fiber [249]. We have also seen an example of a power-center controlling rigid segmentation, when instead of neighboring tribes determining the value of goods through barter or trade, it is the Despot who determines their relative worth by comparing them from on high. But the same abstract machine of power can be found at work in major languages, where the propriety and meaning of statements and words are determined from on high by grammars and dictionaries, instead of by the dynamic expression of existential states and/or successful communication by and/or among speakers. And it is the same abstract machine of power, finally, that measures the value of commodities not via the dynamic regulation of supply and demand among equal trading partners in a free market, but in terms of the amount of labor-power embodied in them in capitalist markets, so that a differential surplus can be extracted from wage-labor through unequal exchange and captured for the sake of capital accumulation.

Having proposed this new distinction between supple and rigid segmentarity, Deleuze & Guattari insist (characteristically) that it is an analytic distinction, and that all societies in fact exhibit both modes:

> Primitive societies have nuclei of rigidity or arborification that as much anticipate the State as ward it off. Conversely, our societies are still suffused by a supple fabric without which their rigid segments would not hold. Supple segmentarity cannot be restricted to primitive peoples. It is not the vestige of the

> savage within us but a perfectly contemporary function... Every society, and every individual, are thus plied by both segmentarities simultaneously: one molar, the other molecular. The configurations differ, for example, between the primitives and us, but the two segmentarities are always in presupposition. In short, everything is political, but every politics is simultaneously a *macropolitics* and a *micropolitics*. [213]

They are therefore intent on preventing possible misunderstandings of the supple/rigid distinction. First of all, supple or molecular segmentary is not necessarily better than rigid segmentation: fascism exhibits supple segmentarity, for example, at a certain stage of its development, before its supple segments start resonating in a shared central black hole of macrofascism. Secondly, the molecular is not imaginary or individual or small-scale, but fully real and social: "...although it is true that the molecular works in detail and operates in small groups, this does not mean that it is any less coextensive with the entire social field than molar organization" [215]. Finally, the molecular does not operate separately from the molar; they always work in tandem, whether in support of or in tension with one another. Thus a policy and program of securitization at the macro level works best and produces the most popular acquiescence when combined with a micropolitics of insecurity. By contrast, it was the hyper-stability of French macropolitics in the 1960s that energized the micropolitics of the student-worker resistance movements of 1968. Political analysis must therefore always proceed on both levels simultaneously: a society can be defined by its contradictions (as Marxism does) only on the level of macropolitics; on the micropolitical level, a society is defined by its lines-of-flight, by whatever "escapes the binary organizations, the resonance apparatus [and] the over-coding machine" operating on the molar level [217]. Both definitions must always be kept in play.

Flows

Having redefined segmentarity in terms of supple-molecular vs. rigid-molar lines, Deleuze & Guattari go on to analyze the molecular level in terms of the quantum flows that subtend molar segmented lines. Thus for example the rigid segmented line matching up a specific dollar amount with a specific commodity (as its price) is accompanied by a flow of the finance-capital that was invested in the production of the commodity and the payment of wages enabling the match-up to begin with. The flow and the line presuppose one another: "the flow and its quanta can be grasped only by virtue of indexes on the segmented line, but conversely, that line and those indexes exist only by virtue of the flow suffusing them" [218]. But they require very different kinds of analysis. In this vein, Deleuze & Guattari contrast the well-known analyses of Emile Durkheim bearing on segmented representations with the less-well known and more important analyses of another French sociologist, Gabriel Tarde, which bear on flows of belief and desire. "Representations... define large-scale [molar] aggregates, or determine segments on a line; beliefs and desires, on the other hand, are flows marked by quanta, flows that are created, exhausted, or transformed, added to one another, subtracted or combined" [219]. A single person or group of people can and should be considered from both perspectives. Classes are molar, for example, while masses are molecular. A single political struggle can even assume two very different aspects, depending on whether it is considered from a molar or a molecular perspective—to the point that even what counts as victory or defeat for a given struggle can differ according to the perspective adopted [221]. Perhaps most important, flows interact with one another in two very different ways: the **connection** of flows increases the force (*puissance*) of both of them, accelerates their shared escape, and augments their quanta, whereas the **conjugation** of flows re-territorializes the lines of flight, bringing them both under the dominance of a single flow that over-codes them [220]. This difference in interaction will become crucial to political strategy, which gets characterized at the very end of the Capture plateau as the construction of "*revolutionary connections* in opposition to the *conjugations of the axiomatic*" [473].

Before moving on to address the issue of power directly, Deleuze & Guattari present a mapping of the three kinds of line and two types of abstract machine resulting from their transformation of the anthropological notion of segmentarity. Using the supple line of primitive segmentarity as a historical point of contrast (rather than a viable option in the present), they distinguish for political purposes between the rigid lines of over-coded State segmentarity and the de-coded and de-territorialized lines of flight mobilizing war-machines. They therefore juxtapose an abstract machine of over-coding—which produces rigid lines, makes their centers resonate, striates homogeneous space, and gets actualized in re-territorializing State assemblages—with an abstract machine of mutation—which draws lines of flight by de-coding and de-territorializing, assures the connection-creation of quantum flows, emits new quanta, and erects war-machines or metamorphosis-machines on its lines-of-flight. Here again, although the two abstract machines are completely different, they are understood to operate always in tandem, producing constant negotiation and oscillation between the molecular and the molar on any given set of lines.

Power

Power as it relates to segmentary lines is defined in terms of three zones. Rigid lines are organized around power-centers that homogenize them and make them readily comparable with one another; this is the zone of power, where the State activates the molar machine of over-coding. Significantly, the State itself is not considered a line or a center, but an apparatus that serves as a resonance-chamber for any number of rigid lines. Rather than being a substantial entity in its own right, then, the State sustains a specific mode of interaction of other entities, acting as a stimulus to or catalyst of their consolidation and amplification. At the same time that a power center organizes a segmented line, it exercises power over a micrological fabric of molecular relations; this is its zone of indiscernibility: "no longer the Schoolmaster but the monitor, the best student, the class dunce, the janitor, etc.... [n]o longer the general, but the junior officers, the noncommissioned officers, the soldier..." [224–5]. Here the control exercised by power-centers varies widely, and it is from this zone, too, that lines-of-flight take their points of departure. Finally and perhaps most importantly, power centers always have a zone of impotence, the quantum flows from which they draw their very strength, yet without ever being able to dominate or control them. The function of the over-coding machine of segmentation is to translate as best it can the flow quanta into rigid line segments, but it never succeeds completely: the quantum flows always contain more virtual potential than can be actually captured and over-coded by the State apparatus. The zone of power of money, for example, is represented by the central bank, which issues and validates currency; its zone of indiscernibility is the aggregate of exchanges actually transacted via the medium of money; and the zone of impotence is the mass of desire for enjoyment in abundance, only a part of which gets captured and converted into commercial transactions.

Deleuze & Guattari end the plateau with an assessment of the four dangers threatening the political lines they have delineated. Two of the four dangers are straightforward: fear makes us embrace the most rigid of lines, and power regularly tries to trap mutation-machines in the over-coding machines of rigid segmentation. But there is also the danger they call "clarity," where supple lines re-territorialize and create "micro-Oedipuses" and "microfascisms," even when they don't resonate in full-fledged macrofascism:

> Instead of the great paranoid fear, we are trapped in a thousand little monomanias, self-evident truths, and clarities that gush from every black hole and no longer form a system, but are only rumble and buzz, blinding lights giving any and everybody the mission of self-appointed judge, dispenser of justice, policeman, neighborhood SS man. [228]

Finally, there is the fourth danger, that lines-of-flight themselves may go bad and turn into lines of abolition and pure destruction; here they cite the murder-suicide of German writer Heinrich von Kleist and Henriette Vogel, along with Hitler's declaration in 1945 that "If the war is lost, may the nation perish" ("Telegram 71," cited 231).

"Treatise on Nomadology—the War Machine" (2)

In *A Thousand Plateaus*, Deleuze & Guattari present two basic human forms of Solution to the Intra-Species Social Organization

Problem: the State and what they call the war-machine. "War-machine" is a peculiar name for the form of social cohesion they also characterize as "nomad," for as I will show, the nomad machine involves war only under very specific circumstances. Indeed, they themselves sometimes call the war-machine an abstract machine of mutation, and Paul Patton has proposed the term "metamorphosis-machine" as a more apt characterization. In any case, the nomad war-machine or mutation-machine and the State are the two main human Intra-Species Social Organization Solutions that Deleuze & Guattari delineate throughout the book, contrasting "war machines of metamorphosis [with] State apparatuses of identity, bands and kingdoms" [360–61]. If it is true that the State-form of social organization receives the lion's share of attention in the book, it is also true that nomadism gets its most complete exposition here in the Nomadology plateau.

To summarize what has been said so far about the State as a stratum and an apparatus, it has been characterized in terms of the following:

- a form of space: striated—along with the propensity to striate all space
- a mode of segmentation: rigid—along with the propensity to establish power-centers in resonance
- a form of science: royal—that also striates space and homogenizes rigid segments
- a semiotic: over-coding—that often operates in concert with striation and rigid segmentation.

Deleuze & Guattari now add that there are two kinds of head-of-State: the magician-king and the jurist-priest, the violent and fearsome Despot and the calm and regulated legislator; and two corresponding modes of social organization: the bond, which is based on obligation, and the pact, which is based on consent. As usual, these are presented as *de jure* categories that always appear *de facto* in mixtures with the prevalence of one alternating with the other. Eventually, a third kind of State-form appears: this is the capitalist State-form, where the State no longer serves as a transcendent over-coding center of resonance, but has become subordinate to capital. The focal point of social organization, that is to say, is no longer the Face of the Despot surrounded by his priests but capital itself, surrounded by its markets. Even the capitalist State, however, retains both of the two basic State-forms, the bond and the pact, and can be seen to oscillate between the predominance of one and the other. What require further explanation now are the concepts of nomadism and the war-machine, and the relations between them. Both of these terms can give rise to considerable confusion—the war-machine because it doesn't always involve war, as I have said, and nomadism because it doesn't refer primarily to nomadic peoples; indeed it owes far more to Greek philosophy than it does to nomads themselves. I begin with the concept of nomadism, before turning to the concept of the war-machine.

Nomadism

Despite the apparent link between nomadism and war in the very title of the plateau, the essence of nomadism lies elsewhere. To the extent that the war-machine is linked to nomadism, Deleuze & Guattari insist, this is "because it is in its essence the constituent element of smooth space, the occupation of this space, displacement within this space, and the corresponding composition of people" [417]. In the same vein, at the very end of the Nomadology plateau, and on precisely the topic of the supplementarity of war vis-à-vis nomadism itself, they insist that even if nomads make war, they do so "only on the condition that they simultaneously create something else, if only new nonorganic social relations" [423]. The principal and positive object of nomadism is therefore not war, but a distinctive composition of social relations occupying smooth space. And it is therefore worth exploring just what this composition of non-organic nomad social relations in smooth space contributes as a Solution to the human Intra-Species Social Organization Problem, especially since it represents an alternative to the better-known State Solution. (Hence the language Deleuze & Guattari deploy of such-and-such "attesting to" the existence of nomadism, found in the first several Propositions of the plateau.)

Are nomadic peoples always organized in a nomadic fashion? That is largely beside the point: for one thing, Deleuze and Guattari's concept of nomadism depends as much (if not more) on the term *nomos* in Greek philosophy (and on its differential relations with *polis* and *logos* [353, 369–73, 384–6]) as on nomadic peoples themselves—whence the importance of rigorously distinguishing between "nomad" as an adjective referring to nomadism in the general sense, and "nomads" as a noun referring to nomadic peoples; for another thing, Deleuze and Guattari say a lot more about the way nomads occupy and move around in smooth space than about the composition of their social relations. Hence the importance of the examples of nomad science, nomad sports, nomad games, and nomad music, which offer insights into this question of the composition of the nomad social field.

In this connection, what Deleuze and Guattari say about science is crucial: "the way in which a science, or a conception of science, participates in the organization of the social field, and in particular induces a division of labor, is part of that science itself" [368–9]. By way of illustration, the same can be said of music: the way in which a practice or a conception of music participates in the composition of the social field and induces a particular division of labor is part of the music itself. So just as Deleuze and Guattari differentiate the journeymen's plane of consistency from the architects' plane of organization, and nomad science from royal science, I will according to the same criteria distinguish nomad music—that is to say, improvisational jazz—from royal or classical music. Briefly, the three basic criteria are as follows:

1) In nomad science, there is indeed a technical division of labor—the differentiation of activities, the specialization of functions—but there is no political division of labor that would place certain positions or functions above others (e.g. architects over stone-masons). Royal science, by contrast, entails a disqualification of manual labor in favor of intellectual labor, and thereby superimposes a political division of labor—hierarchy, power differentials, distinctions of prestige and remuneration—on the technical division of labor.

2) At the same time, royal science institutes a separation between conception and execution. With the emergence of royal science, an artisan class where conception and execution coincided in the same person gave way to a proletarian working class of unskilled labor faced with

a scientific class holding a monopoly of knowledge and control. "The State does not give power (*pouvoir*) to the intellectual or conceptual innovators; on the contrary, it makes them a strictly dependent organ with an autonomy that is only imagined, yet is sufficient to divest of all of their power (*puissance*) those whose job it becomes simply to reproduce or implement [the instructions issued to them]" [368]. The same is true for music. In a symphony orchestra performing classical music, conception is sharply separated from execution: musicians merely reproduce a program created in advance by the genius-composer, and what's more, they play at the command of the orchestra conductor. In jazz improvisation, by contrast, conception and execution coincide in the same personnel and at the same time—they make it up as they go along, in a process of creative itineration rather than slavish re-iteration—and there is no need for a conductor.

3) Jazz improvisation perfectly illustrates a third criterion of nomad science and of the nomad body politic in general—the criterion Deleuze and Guattari adapt from Gilbert Simondon which distinguishes nomad composition from hylomorphic organization [555n. 33]. It is not only that nomad music and science operate by creative itineration rather than by reproductive repetition (of a score or an alleged law of nature), as we have seen; it is also that they remain sensitive to the singularities of sound-substance, physical substance, biological substance, and so on. Each musical key has a special tonality, and therefore presents distinctive possibilities for composition or improvisation. Moreover, a "wrong note"—or rather, an **unexpected** note—played by a jazz musician is not necessarily a mistake—as it would most certainly be if it were played by a classical musician—inasmuch as the other musicians in the group can always incorporate it as a singularity into the piece they are improvising. In the smooth space of musical improvisation, it is never a question of imposing form on a passive, inert substance: neither the substance of sound nor of human beings, neither the musical keys nor the musicians are passive. Instead, there is a process

of spontaneous structuration where a certain singular coherence or consistency emerges which is not imposed by either a conductor or a score, but remains absolutely immanent to the creative activity of the group. A nomad body politic follows immanent rules (*nomoi*) which are for the most part implicit, rather than obeying laws (*logoi*) that are formulated explicitly and/or imposed from above by a transcendent agent or agency [369–74].

The concept of nomadism, in sum, hinges on the notion that **the manner in which forms of human activity contribute to the organization of the social field, and in particular the way in which they induce a certain division of labor or not (political vs. technical, intellectual vs. manual), constitutes an intrinsic part of that activity itself.** Nomadism thus designates forms of human activity where the social field remains a smooth space; where modes and principles of social organization arise immanently from group activity itself, instead of being imposed by a transcendent instance from above; where itinerant following of singularities and group creation prevail over the reproduction and/or imposition of preexisting forms and the issuing and obeying of commands. It should be understood that this is a heuristic distinction: few real instances of human activity will appear purely immanent or purely transcendent. But it is the components of this concept that guide nomadology in mapping various instances of nomadism and assessing their potential for creative rather than mechanical repetition, for mutually reinforcing intersections, and for widespread social transformation.

War-machines

Turning now to the concept of the war-machine, while its consistency derives from its focus on a specific form of sociality as a Solution to the human Intra-Species Social Organization Problem, its scope of variation is wide: indeed "[t]he first theoretical element of importance," Deleuze & Guattari insist, "is the fact that the war machine has many varied meanings" [422], and some of that variation arises from the fact that some war-machines have war as their object or aim, and some do not. There are in fact no fewer than six very different variants of the war-machine in *A Thousand Plateaus*, among which it is crucial to make careful distinctions. Moreover, in addition to ascertaining the different variants of the concept, it is important to identify and distinguish its four key components: aim, object, space (smooth vs. striated), and form-of-sociality (ultimately hinging on the distinction between denumerable and non-denumerable sets, developed in the Capture plateau).

Two of the six variants have very little to do with war. Indeed, the first variant barely merits the name war-machine, inasmuch as it does not have war as its object at all: its essence is a rhizomatic or nomadic form of social relations operating in smooth space [417], and its objectives can be as varied as "building bridges or cathedrals or rendering judgments or making music or instituting a science, a technology" [366]. The main reason for using the term war-machine here is the transformative nature of these activities, along with the nomadic nature of the social relations involved. A second variant—the "war-machine of revolutionary movement"—may involve a struggle to "construct **revolutionary connections** in opposition to the **conjugations of the [capitalist] axiomatic**" [473; see also 220, 464], as we shall see, but this is not a war (as conventionally understood), it may not necessarily entail violence, and in any case, its ultimate aim is to render **all** social relations nomadic through the "minoritarian becoming-everything of everybody" [473, transmod]. Nomadic bands only begin to justify the "war" component of the term "war-machine" in the concept's third variant, where they do indeed take on war itself as their object—in opposition to the State, with the aim of protecting or rescuing their smooth space from State striation. This is essentially a tactical war (in the sense Michel de Certeau derives from von Clausewitz), fought against the State's strategic aim of incorporating all available open space into its territory. The State pursues this strategy by mobilizing the war-machine in its fourth variant, when it has been appropriated as a means to serve the State's essentially **political** ends: the aim of securing, striating, protecting, and expanding State territory. While these four variants are essentially typological, the last two are historical, and reference the mid–20th century transformations of limited war into total war, and then of the war-machine's political aims into economic aims—both of which occurred in connection with the rise and fall of Nazism and the subsequent emergence of the Cold War (the crux of geo-politics at the time Deleuze & Guattari wrote *A Thousand Plateaus*).

The State war-machine (our fourth variant) always has war as its exclusive object (it must constantly protect, if not expand, its territory), yet it remains subordinate to the State's political aims: in this context, war is merely "the continuation of politics by other means" (von Clausewitz, cited by Deleuze & Guattari [467]), and it is still only limited war. The fifth variant of the war-machine, which is historical fascism, serves for Deleuze & Guattari as a transition from the fourth variant to the sixth: fascism is what transformed limited war into total war, paving the way for the totalizing war-machine of global capitalism. But in the process of transformation, a fundamental change in the aim of the war-machine takes place. The Nazi war-machine came to power by promising Germany an economic and social rebirth after the devastating feat of the First World War. It was able to deliver on this promise, given the importance of heavy industry for the German economy (as for most advanced economies in the 20th century) and for Hitler's rise to power, only by linking economic expansion with military conquest. Only the transformation of limited war into total war would both keep the wheels of industry turning and mobilize continuing popular support for the Nazi regime. At this point, a critical ambiguity arises regarding the aims of war: is the political goal of world conquest driving economic expansion, or is the economic imperative of constant expansion driving the political goal of conquest? The same question could be asked about the United States at the time: did entering the war to defend a free Europe stimulate the economy, or did stimulating the flagging New Deal economy prompt the decision to enter the war? No doubt both. But the point is that war became—and remains to this day—a nearly perfect solution to the classical capitalist crisis of overproduction: industry produces the armaments for State warfare, which then demolishes them, which in turn requires the production of new armaments—and so on, ad infinitum. Eventually—as United States General-become-President Eisenhower was the first to express in a slogan of crystalline clarity—the economic imperatives of "the military-industrial complex" would supersede the political imperatives of the State: capital accumulation becomes the true aim of the war-machine, and territorial expansion or control becomes at most merely one possible object, and no longer a necessary one. Colonialism gives way to neo-colonialism. Hot war gives way to cold war: territory no longer has to change hands or even be at stake for a nuclear arms race to boost capital accumulation on a massive scale.

With global capitalism, the war-machine in its sixth variant has escaped the grasp of the State and now envelops it, with the State now serving merely as a variable model of realization for capitalist axiomatization. Here, capital accumulation as the aim of the sixth war-machine exceeds the control of the State and pervades society totally (that is, extensively as well as intensively: via globalization as well as real subsumption), with its economic imperatives subordinating political ends, without of course doing away with politics altogether. State politics and diplomacy, even war itself, are now merely the continuation of capital accumulation by other means, as it were. The aim of the global-capitalist war-machine, according to Deleuze & Guattari, is no longer hot war (as means to an end furnished by the State) but capital accumulation itself, which at the time they wrote took the form of a cold war of deterrence in which the State-administered welfare system and military-industrial complex came to function as little more than political means serving ultimately economic ends [467]. But the global-capitalist war-machine has taken a variety of different forms since, often summed up by terms like neo-liberal securitization. Identifying global capitalism as a war-machine enables us to understand how different, how much faster and more flexible, its process of axiomatization is from the over-coding and striating procedures of State power, even though capitalism still uses states as models of realization for the re-territorializing moment of its axiomatic. We learn more about the third, capitalist State-form in the Apparatus of Capture plateau, where the initial emergence and subsequent transformations of capitalism are also examined in more detail.

"Apparatus of Capture" (2)

Like the Micropolitics and Segmentarity plateau, the Capture plateau makes several strong interventions, here in the field of political economy rather than political anthropology. One important challenge involves the origins of money: as we have already seen (in the anthro-ethology section), money first arose as a form of payment of imperial tribute and State taxes, not as a medium of commercial exchange. A similar assertion of the primacy of State politics over economics affects the status of the Marxist concept of modes of production. For while orthodox Marxism claims that the State is determined by the mode of production, Deleuze & Guattari show that it was Despotic State stockpiles (of land, labor, and money) that made undifferentiated work-activity into labor, and production into a mode, in the first place [429]. They then go on to assert categorically that "we [should] define social formations by *machinic processes* and not by modes of production ([for] these on the contrary depend on the processes)" [435]. The point is not that modes of production don't exist, for they clearly do, but that they are to be understood as effects rather than causes—that is to say, as the contingent result of assemblage of machinic processes, not as determining entities or unities in their own right.

The Capture plateau also intervenes in what might be called the theory of history, in this respect aligning very closely with Foucault's theory and practice of "discontinuous history." Deleuze & Guattari refuse to give an account of the emergence of the Despotic State-form, other than to say that it appeared "in a single stroke" [427, 428, 448] with the violent conquest of one or more peoples by a Despot or emperor. They do not deny that there are tendencies toward centralization in primitive-territorial social formations, but these tendencies are visible primarily in the mechanisms by which those societies precisely ward them off and prevent a State from forming (as we saw in the anthro-ethology section). This refusal of any evolutionary account of the emergence of the State underscores the initial and on-going violence (conquest, policing, the death-sentence) that lie at the heart of the State-form. In a similar vein, Deleuze & Guattari refuse any evolutionary account of the emergence of capitalism: it too arose "in a single stroke" [453] through the contingent encounter of disposable (liquid) wealth in the form of money and disposable labor-power in the form of destitute people. Here, too, they underscore the accidental nature of this encounter in order to prevent capitalism from appearing naturally or necessarily the dominant mode of production it now seems to be. That having been said, their account of the fortuitous emergence of capitalism in early modern Europe is quite intricate, and it is important (among other reasons) for the understanding of contemporary globalizing capitalism it affords.

How the State enables capitalism

Three factors explain the emergence of capitalism. The chance encounter just mentioned between wealth and labor is one: "Capitalism forms when the flow of unqualified wealth encounters the flow of unqualified labor and conjugates with it" [453]. This conjugation of liquid ("unqualified") wealth in money form with "free" (unqualified) labor-power (i.e. not owned by or beholden to a master or lord) constitutes the first and fundamental axiom of what Deleuze & Guattari call the capitalist axiomatic. Unlike savage and despotic societies, which organize society qualitatively via codes and over-codes, the capitalist mode of production organizes society quantitatively via axiomatization, by conjugating in the first place de-coded flows of wealth and de-territorialized flows of labor-power in order to produce surplus-value, which is then privately appropriated by capitalists. Money is crucial to the de-coding of wealth, which henceforth exists in a purely abstract and, as we have seen, an infinitely accumulable form. Similarly, the de-territorializing process of removing labor-power from pre-existing means of life—a process Marx referred to somewhat sarcastically as "primitive accumulation," but which might be better called primitive or prior destitution—is equally crucial to the emergence of capitalism in this first axiom: de-territorialized labor-power is obliged to sell itself for wages in order to survive. And this labor-power is "unqualified" or abstract in that it is a pure **virtual** potential to work that is given in exchange to the capitalist—not a surplus product (or its money equivalent), such as gets paid in tribute to the Despot. Indeed, one of the truly remarkable features of the capitalist mode of production is that the "unqualified" flows of abstract wealth and labor-potential take on concrete form only **after** they are conjugated by the investment of capital—only after the decision has been made, for example, to invest in wool thread and mechanical looms and to hire and train former peasants or serfs to operate them. Capitalists make decisions in the **virtual** realm, that is to say, before **actual** production and consumption ever take place. As we saw in an earlier section, money is the form of expression that is most completely independent of all content-planes, even more than language. But in the form of capital, money eventually becomes the very basis for social organization (the kind of basis that was called a "socius" in *Anti-Oedipus*). If, as I have suggested, expressive motifs and the cub's-play of wolves represent first steps toward access to the virtual, the advent of capitalism represents a quantum leap in the same direction. And once the capitalist conjugation of flows of liquid wealth and free labor-power becomes self-sustaining, capital continues to expand by axiomatizing all kinds of other abstract flows: flows of natural resources, flows of consumer taste, flows of increasingly complex human abilities (job skills), flows of scientific knowledge and technological know-how, and so on. And as capitalism develops, axioms can be added or subtracted at will; capital becomes a probe-head (like evolution): whatever works to produce surplus-value, so long as the core axiom emerging from the initial encounter of wealth and labor-power continues to function.

Even though the State will henceforth become subordinate to the imperatives and experiments of capitalist axiomatization, the initial encounter took place in a context where the State played two essential enabling roles. The first involved the constitution of stockpiles, discussed in the earlier section on anthro-ethology—the stockpiles of land, labor, and money that enabled the infinite accumulation of wealth in the forms of ground-rent, surplus-product, and tribute. Capitalism transforms the relations among these three stockpiles significantly, in the process referred to—albeit in very different ways—by Adam Smith and Karl Marx as "primitive accumulation." The ownership of land and the ownership or immediate (i.e. not mediated by money) appropriation of surplus-labor (i.e. via slavery or serfdom) diminish in importance or disappear altogether. Rent now accrues to owners of any form of capital (not just land), and the appropriation of surplus now takes an indirect form, as wage-slavery replaces slavery per se—that is to say, as surplus is appropriated in the form of surplus-value rather than surplus-product, in a process mediated crucially by money, which conjugates a mass quantity of wages with an always slightly different mass quantity of commodities in such a way that a differential surplus can be extracted. Tribute, finally, is transformed into interest, as State-sanctioned central banks take over the responsibility for issuing and validating currencies, and the infinite debt formerly owed to the Despot transfers over to the infinite debt owed to capital itself.

The second role of the State in the chance emergence of capitalism is in one sense even more significant, in that both its initial contribution and its eventual disappearance are crucial to understanding the capitalist mode of production and its historical transmutations: the State initially provided what Deleuze & Guattari call a space of "intraconsistency" of vertically hierarchized elements resonating with a center that exists "behind" or "on top" of them rather than in the midst of them [433]. This intraconsistency contrasts with the space of "transconsistency" characteristic of the pre- or para- State relations among towns, which form a horizontal network cohering via the logic of "among" (with...with...with...). Ultimately, Deleuze & Guattari insist, "it was through the State-form and not the town-form that capitalism triumphed" [434]—at first. Yet once it passes a critical threshold of accumulation, capitalism overspills the intraconsistent space furnished to it by the State, and starts operating in the transconsistent space of the world market, as we shall see.

How capitalism subsumes the State

But first I need to examine how thoroughly capitalism transforms the State in subordinating it to its own imperative of private capital accumulation. Due to the superior de-territorializating force of high-speed capital, it re-territorializes on states, which henceforth function very differently from the Despotic State and its faciality-machine. For one thing, capitalist or axiomatizing states become responsible for the black-hole subjectification of populations according to the ever-changing demands of high-speed capital: job-training, census-taking, and enforcing neo-liberalism are all facets of subjectification undertaken by the State for the sake of capital. At the same time, states assume responsibility for the white-wall constitution of a unified national market with a single, stable currency. Of the two major State-forms, the Despotic "bond" form tends to be eclipsed (not eliminated) by the "pact" form, as so-called civil society and the public sphere develop and the supposedly "free" citizen prevails over (without completely obliterating) the politically bound subject. Now, instead of over-coding already coded flows for the glory of the Despot, the function of the State is to orchestrate the conjugation of increasingly de-coded quantum flows of raw materials and processes, untrained labor-power and purchasing-power, technologies, and so on.

Ultimately, however, a tipping-point is reached where the speed and power of capital to conjugate or axiomatize de-coded flows surpasses the power of the State to over-code coded flows, and states become mere models of realization and spaces of re-territorialization for the capitalist axiomatic, which now spans the globe. States now replace towns as the elements of a transconsistent network of global rather than regional or national scope, and in which they also function as mobile nodes enabling the comparison of national currencies on the white wall of now-global markets in the service of speculative finance capital. The black-hole subjectification of populations, meanwhile, gives way to the resurgence of a machinic enslavement reminiscent of the slave labor employed by the first great mega-machine of capture and accumulation, the Despotic State. Whereas subjectified workers use technical machines in the process of producing commodities, workers and consumers get machinically enslaved when they—or rather, various segments of their activities—become parts of a social machine devoted to the accumulation of capital anywhere and everywhere throughout social life (which Deleuze would later call "control society"[9]). In this context, as now-global capital engulfs states as models of realization for private accumulation, the regime of subjectification appears as a mere temporary transitional stage between the first great mega-machine of capture, Despotism, and the second, which is global capitalism itself—both of which operate by machinic enslavement.

The superior de-territorializing power of capital arises from two factors: the degree of autonomy and abstraction of its formalization of expression—money—and the fact that capitalist axiomatization operates directly on de-coded quantum flows, not on coded or over-coded line-segments. Liquid money and abstract labor-power are among the most significant of such flows, but so are the flows of matter and energy accessed through technologies, the flows of desire and belief managed through marketing and politics, and so on. Capital has the capacity to reach out its pincers and grab hold of the plane of consistency directly, in places that **subsequently** become strata serving one or more of its axioms. Capital thus affords unprecedented access to the domain of the virtual, which it explores as an experimental probe-head operating at increasingly high speed—a speed surpassed only by the theoretically infinite speed of philosophical thought itself. Crucial to the power of capitalist axiomatization—and even more critical to our understanding of it—is the fact that it conjugates and connects these de-coded flows **simultaneously**. Conjugation, as we saw in the Micropolitics plateau [220], limits and re-territorializes flows by bringing them under the dominance of a power center that over-codes them. Connection, by contrast, increases the force of flows by increasing their escape-velocities and augmenting their quanta. What Deleuze & Guattari call the "undecidability" of capitalist axiomatization is precisely that it does both at the same time. By connecting flows, capitalism continually "revolutionizes the forces of production," as Marx and Engels put it, yet at the same time by conjugating them it captures surplus-value for black-hole private accumulation which knows no limits: "the deepest law of capitalism [is that] it continually sets and then repels its own limits, but in so doing gives rise to numerous flows in all directions that escape its axiomatic" [472]. And the reason that so many flows inevitably escape axiomatization is that it can only operate on segmented lines, on what Deleuze & Guattari here refer to as "denumerable sets" [472 passim]. Since, as we have seen, all power-centers entail a zone of impotence as well as a zone of power, and since capital's formalization of expression involves abstract quantification in money-terms, its zone of impotence is comprised of any and all elements, flows, and relations that cannot be denumerated or quantified: "*At the same time as capitalism is effectuated in the denumerable sets serving as its models, it necessarily constitutes nondenumerable sets that cut across and disrupt those models*" [472]. Therefore, the core slogan or imperative for politics will be to "construct *revolutionary connections* in opposition to the *conjugations of the axiomatic*" [473].

Becoming and Revolution

Politics for Deleuze & Guattari is therefore situated, I would say, at the intersection—and, more importantly, the point of divergence—of the conjugations and the connections resulting from capitalist axiomatization: for capital

> does not effect the "conjugation" of the de-territorialized and decoded flows without those flows forging farther ahead;

without their escaping both the axiomatic that conjugates them and the models that re-territorialize them; without their tending to enter into "connections" that delineate a new Land... [472].

In the preceding chapter on Ethics, I distinguished categorically between becoming-minoritarian and being-(in)-a-minority; I can now add that "what is proper to the minority is to assert a power of the nondenumerable" [470]. To be sure, Deleuze & Guattari acknowledge that minority politics often does, and indeed often must, challenge the State and capital at the level of the axiomatic, and seek to change it to their own benefit:

> Once again, this is not to say that the struggle on the level of the axioms is without importance; on the contrary, it is determining (at the most diverse levels: women's struggle for the vote, for abortion, for jobs; the struggle of the regions for autonomy; the struggle of the Third World; the struggle of the oppressed masses and minorities in the East or West...). But there is also always a sign to indicate that these struggles are the index of another, coexistent combat. However modest the demand, it always constitutes a point that the axiomatic cannot tolerate: when people demand to formulate their problems themselves... [470-1]

And formulating Problems, we should recall in passing, is the hallmark of both nomad science and political philosophy itself. But the struggle of denumerable sets for rights and redress and so forth is only half the battle—and not the better half, so to speak. Beneath the molar struggle over axioms, there are always other, micropolitical struggles, the best of which instantiate the minoritarian becoming-everything of everybody. Indeed, not only are political struggles always double (axiomatic/minoritarian), but so is history itself: any historical event always contains both a linear development controlled by a power center such as the State and a set of potential becomings aimed in multiple directions orthogonal or transversal to that line of historical development. There is thus a fundamental difference between State history and the minoritarian becomings unleashed by capitalism: whereas the State continually adds developments to its past, both in writing and through territorial conquest, a minoritarian becoming (as "anti-memory") subtracts the codifications of its past in order to reach the plane of consistency containing the maximum potential for taking history in other directions. In other words, the narratives of State history and the actions informed by that history retrace and reinforce the causal chains that produced and/or consolidate State rule—this is one sense in which history is always written by the victor. Minoritarian becomings, by contrast, strip away (or de-code) the actual determinations of the past, and restore to the present its virtual potential to become-otherwise in the future. So one of the central tasks of political philosophy is precisely to map all minoritarian becomings, in order to ascertain where their immanent potential lies for propitious change. And if becoming-minoritarian assumes a "universal figure," as Deleuze & Guattari explicitly say it does [470], it is both because everyone is potentially involved, as we saw in the Linguistics plateau [106], and because everyone has the potential to become-imperceptible, as we saw in the Becomings plateau.

But minoritarian becomings are not the only universal: there is also the worldwide market—which, as Deleuze & Guattari say in *What is Philosophy?*, is "the only thing that is universal in capitalism" [*What is Philosophy?* p. 106]. As the highest-speed vector of de-territorialization and the most abstract formalization of expression, the world market offers the greatest virtual potential as a Solution to the human Intra-Species Social Organization Problem. But of course, that potential is not only limited by capital, it is in fact converted back into oppression, exploitation, and immiseration by capital. And inasmuch as the struggle over the virtual potential of the world market thereby assumes paramount importance, "the power of minority... finds its figure or its universal consciousness in the proletariat" [472]. The power of capital as mega-machine of capture and infinite private accumulation depends on axiomatizing flows that are denumerable, but it does so at the cost of producing its own zone of impotence containing the multitude of flows that remain nondenumerable. In this light, the political imperative is to connect and assemble some of these flows to constitute "a war machine whose aim is neither the war of extermination [e.g. Nazi Germany] nor the peace of generalized terror [e.g. the Cold War], but revolutionary movement (the connection of flows, the composition of nondenumerable aggregates, the minoritarian becoming-everything of everybody)"

[472–3]. So go ahead: become-minoritarian, everybody! Make love, not war! Make your loves into war-machines, and convert your wars into love-machines! And fire the boss! And cancel the infinite debt! And break some conjugations! And make some more connections! And...

CODA

So this reading of *A Thousand Plateaus* is now complete. In this performance, I have been as faithful to the book as possible—I played it straight, no chaser—save in one respect: the matter of style. Deleuze & Guattari gave their rendition of the book a circular form—only for laughs, they said, but also for other reasons, as we saw: to make the book a rhizome, going off in multiple directions at once. I, however, have given my rendition a linear form—partly for reasons of modesty, simplicity, and accessibility, but for another reason as well. To inspire some enthusiasm. A book like this is not just a rhizome, designed as a patchwork-map of the world's many becomings: it is a war-machine, intended to transform it. So this reading began at the very beginning—with the Big Bang!—proceeded segment by segment through epistemology, ontology, and anthropology to ethics and then politics—and ends in exhortation. Of the three related yet distinct dimensions of the plane of consistency—the aesthetic, the ethical, and the political—it culminates in the political, in order to bring the transformative force of the war-machine to bear in the widest possible arena. Other readings could equally well foreground the transformative tendencies of aesthetics or ethics. In any case, at their most successful, war-machines assemble packs, and they always operate only through contagion or inspiration. So let this reading go viral! For the point of doing philosophy, echoes a familiar refrain, is not merely to interpret the world, but to experiment and improvise with it, and ultimately to change it—for the better.

CHAPTER FOUR

Reception and Influence

Mapping the reception and influence of a book such as *A Thousand Plateaus* is a difficult task for two principal reasons. For one thing, the book is, as we have seen, extraordinarily wide-ranging, and its influence has been equally so. For another, this book is one among several that were co-authored by Deleuze & Guattari, each of whom also wrote a number of books on their own—and so segregating the influence of this one book from the more general influence of Deleuze & Guattari and of Deleuze and Guattari themselves becomes virtually impossible. One plausible measure of the influence of *A Thousand Plateaus* itself is the fact that in the three decades following its initial publication (in 1980) it was translated into no fewer than nine languages: English (1987), Italian (1987), German (1992), Spanish (1997), Swedish (1998), Danish (2005), Portuguese (2007), Chinese (2010) and Japanese (2010). But this apparently simple fact calls for careful contextualization.

The fact that the English and Italian translations appeared the same year, for instance, can be misleading. Because of Guattari's personal connection with Italy's very strong political autonomy and anti-psychiatry movements, *Anti-Oedipus* had been translated into Italian in 1975 (just three years after its initial publication in 1972), and met with immediate success. By the time of *A Thousand Plateaus*, however, the political situation in Italy had changed dramatically, and although a selection of four plateaus ("Rhizome," "How Do You Make Yourself a Body Without Organs?," "On the Refrain," and "Apparatus of Capture") appeared in Italian immediately (1980), the full translation didn't appear until 1987, and it was greeted with general indifference, especially among academics. The important exception here is the political activist and theorist Antonio Negri, who shared with Deleuze an interest in Spinoza, and whose later collaborative work with American Michael Hardt would draw on Deleuze & Guattari (along with Foucault and a plethora of other figures). Negri would co-author a book with Guattari, *Communists Like Us*, the year before the latter's final collaboration with Deleuze. Negri aside, it was only toward the end of the century that more widespread interest in Deleuze & Guattari re-emerged in Italy, and then (in large part thanks to the journal *Millepiani*) it was largely among artists, architects, urban sociologists and geographers, and city planners. (The signal exception here is Italian philosopher Maurizio Lazzarato, whose insightful book on Deleuze & Guattari, *Les Révolutions du capitalisme*, has yet to be translated into English.) The English translation of *A Thousand Plateaus*, by contrast, served and fostered a more or less continuously growing community of scholars spread across three continents (Australia, the British Isles, and North America), and it is fair to say that Deleuze & Guattari's influence in the English-speaking world has far exceeded their impact in France. Early on, Deleuze & Guattari's work was integrated in Australia into the emerging field of cultural studies, largely due to work in philosophy by Paul Patton and in cultural and literary studies by Meaghan Morris and by Ian Buchanan, who organized a Deleuze symposium at the University of Western Australia in 1996, and has since become editor of both the journal *Deleuze Studies* and of Deleuze book series devoted to Deleuze at the Edinburgh University Press. In Great Britain, the University of Warwick sponsored early conferences on Deleuze & Guattari, organized by Keith Ansell-Pearson and Nick Land; now, Manchester Metropolitan University hosts a Deleuze Studies network along with an online journal called *A/V*. In North America, meanwhile, it was Sylvère Lotringer at Columbia, and then communications scholar Lawrence Grossberg and Canadian philosopher Constantin Boundas who spurred interest in Deleuze & Guattari, with Lotringer sponsoring an early (and ill-fated) New York conference in 1975, featuring Deleuze and Guattari themselves, and devoting several issues of his journal *Semiotext(e)* to translations of their work; Grossberg introducing their work into the field of cultural studies; and Boundas producing translations of several of Deleuze's earlier philosophical works, editing a number of important collections on Deleuze's philosophy, and organizing (with the help of Dorothea Olkowski from the University of Colorado) a series of ground-breaking conferences at Trent University (in 1992, 1996, 1999, and 2004), each one bigger than the last. Conversely, the translation of *A Thousand Plateaus* into Portuguese appears surprisingly late, given that Brazil's reception and development of schizoanalysis, first proposed in *Anti-Oedipus*, was by far the most extensive of anywhere in the world, thanks in part to frequent visits there by Guattari and by one of Deleuze's most important French students, Eric Alliez, along with work by Suely Rolnik, a psychoanalyst and professor at the Catholic University of São Paolo. In any case, the translations of *A Thousand Plateaus* provide one index of the book's importance around the world, even if the extent of its influence has varied considerably according to time and place.

In France, meanwhile, the reception of *A Thousand Plateaus* was more subdued. *Anti-Oedipus* had been difficult to assimilate to the relatively rigid structures of the French academy—and the same was even more true of *Kafka* and *A Thousand Plateaus*. An assemblage of mutual influence and rivalry connected Deleuze & Guattari with a number of important French intellectuals of their day, including Louis Althusser, Maurice Blanchot, Jacques Derrida, Michel Foucault, Pierre Klossowski, Jacques Lacan and Jean-François Lyotard, among others. As early as *Difference and Repetition*, Deleuze had expressed complete agreement with Althusser's reading of Marx, particularly with the notion that a mode of production is to be understood as a structure that poses problems which social formations solve in various ways. Late in his career, in turn, Althusser acknowledged the importance of Deleuze in developing what Althusser called a "materialism of the encounter." Althusser even adapted Deleuze & Guattari's category of "becoming" to designate the contingency of a mode of production's ability to reproduce itself: a mode of production doesn't obey necessary laws; such laws are always only "becoming-necessary," without ever arriving at absolute necessity. Jacques Derrida, meanwhile, declared at the time of Deleuze's death that he always felt in complete agreement with Deleuze's writings (even though Deleuze's stance was very different, and not nearly as textual or linguo-centric as Derrida's). The reciprocal influences between Deleuze and Foucault and Deleuze and Lyotard (they were colleagues at Vincennes) are so extensive as to be almost impossible to unravel, even if the men themselves eventually drifted apart. Lyotard's book on *Libidinal Economy* (1974) appeared shortly after *Anti-Oedipus* (1972), and reflected the same desire to renew political thinking by confronting political economy with psychoanalysis, and vice versa. Foucault's historical studies of different forms of power (sovereign vs. disciplinary power, for instance) are comparable to Deleuze & Guattari's modes of libidinal production (*Anti-Oedipus*) and regimes of signs (*A Thousand Plateaus*), and Deleuze is explicit about developing Foucault's reflections on disciplinary power to account for a new form of power, in his famous late essay on "control society."

Then there are former students and younger colleagues. Students of Deleuze's and/or Guattari's work such as Jean-Clet Martin and Eric Alliez produced important overviews, and extended their thinking further in domains such as the plastic arts (in the case of Alliez). Belgian philosopher Isabelle Stengers drew extensively on Deleuze & Guattari for her work on the philosophy of science. In the same field, Bruno Latour's work, particularly his notion of hybrid objects (machinic assemblages) that are neither purely social nor purely natural but both, and Donna Haraway's "Cyborg Manifesto," both reflect the influence of Deleuze & Guattari (although they may not be as explicit in acknowledging it as Stengers is), as does the field of "posthumanism" more generally. The scope and analytic apparatus of French economist Jacques Attali's *Noise: the Political Economy of Music* resemble those of *Capitalism and Schizophrenia*, although it appeared (in French) before *A Thousand Plateaus*. Rosi Braidotti, Distinguished University Professor and founding Director of the Centre for the Humanities at Utrecht University has written extensively on feminism, philosophy and ethics from a Deleuzo-Guattarian perspective. Patricia Pisters, professor and chair of Media Studies at the University of Amsterdam, develops Deleuze's work on philosophy and film in her work on neuro-biology and contemporary screen culture. French media scholar Pierre Lévy draws directly on Deleuze & Guattari in his analyses of digitally-mediated 'collective intelligence' and virtual reality. Anne Sauvagnargues, philosophy professor at the University of Paris X, has pursued the complex relations of Deleuze & Guattari's thought to both art and music (among other things), while Richard Pinhas, a close friend of Deleuze, has composed music inspired by Deleuze & Guattari. Pinhas also established and maintains a website dedicated to making transcripts of Deleuze's courses at Vincennes (practically all of which Pinhas himself attended) available to Deleuze & Guattari scholars around the globe.

Responses to *A Thousand Plateaus* were by no means unanimously positive, however.[1] Before the English translation of the book appeared, Alice Jardine challenged the notion of "becoming-woman" on the grounds that it might eliminate the political agency of real women altogether—despite Deleuze & Guattari's insistence that alongside becoming-woman, it remains "indispensable for women to conduct a molar politics, with a view to winning back their own organism, their own history, their own subjectivity" [276]. Subsequently, feminist scholars including Rosi Braidotti, Claire Colebrook, Elizabeth Grosz and Tasmin Lorraine have drawn extensively on Deleuze & Guattari to advance feminist theorization of the body, agency, gender, and/or sexuality, among other things. After devoting a chapter to Deleuze in her first book, Judith Butler developed a ground-breaking theory of gender performance which has been influential in both feminist and queer studies, whereby the gendered subject emerges as a product or by-product of repetition, and the degree of difference in repetition—ranging from bare repetition to masquerade—determines whether a subject reinforces or subverts normative gender roles.

Even more strenuously than Jardine, Alan Sokal and Jean Bricmont objected to the recourse made throughout *A Thousand Plateaus* to science and mathematics, devoting an entire chapter of their book, *Fashionable Nonsense*, to Deleuze & Guattari. Important work by Manuel DeLanda, Brian Massumi, Arkady Plotnitsky, John Protevi, and Brian Rotman, however—not to repeat mention of the work of Stengers and Stengers & Prigogine—has shown how important mathematics and science are to Deleuze & Guattari, and how the significance and relevance of recent advances in science can be illuminated in turn by the metaphysics presented in *A Thousand Plateaus*. DeLanda's work, however, fails to distinguish clearly between science and philosophy, and therefore ends up turning Deleuze & Guattari's rhizomatics into mere social science—despite their repeated insistence that philosophical concepts (unlike scientific functions) are not referential. Indeed the failure to distinguish among the various components of Deleuze & Guattari's metaphysics is all too common. Christopher Miller, for example, attacks their notion of "nomadism" as a misrepresentation of nomadic peoples, mistaking a self-referential, pragmatic philosophical concept for a referential social-scientific (anthropological or ethnographic) one. Peter Hallward makes a similar mistake, confusing the ultimate aesthetic imperative (becoming-imperceptible) with the eminently practical, down-to-earth imperatives of ethics and politics. Ironically enough, even the aesthetic imperative of becoming-imperceptible, which he considers part and parcel of the "other-worldly" orientation of all of Deleuze & Guattari's thought, in fact links becomings with *haecceities*, as we have seen, and it is hard to imagine anything more "this-worldly" than the "this-here-now" of a *haecceity*.

In the field of **science**, Deleuze & Guattari's influence is most clearly felt in the research programs of Manuel DeLanda, Brian Massumi and John Protevi. Elizabth Grosz's work connects the life sciences with **aesthetics**, where Ronald Bogue, Stephen Shaviro and Stephen Zepke have also done important work. Within the field of aesthetics, architecture has seen a surprising amount of Deleuze-inspired work, largely because of Deleuze's adaptation of the architectural image of thought in his later book on Leibniz (*The Fold*), but also because of the emphasis on space in *A Thousand Plateaus*. (On Deleuze and architecture, see works by Ballantyne, Brott, Frichot and Grosz, Karatani and Stoner.) It is also surprising that more has not been done with painting, given Deleuze & Guattari's treatment of it, while Deleuze's considerable influence in film studies is due almost entirely to his later two-volume cinema study of the movement- and time-images (whereas *A Thousand Plateaus* focuses more on space, as we have seen). *Cultural Critique* devoted two entire issues to the concept of minor literature proposed in the *Kafka* book, but the influence of *A Thousand Plateaus* on literary studies has been relatively slight—here again partly because of the importance of Deleuze's own collection, *Essays Critical and Clinical*—with the important exceptions of Ronald Bogue, whose *Deleuze's Way* links aesthetics and ethics in literature and the other arts and whose *Deleuzian Fabulation* is devoted to literature; and of French Professor of English Jean-Jacques Lecercle, whose work spans linguistics, philosophy and literary studies in ways that are explicitly indebted to Deleuze & Guattari.

In the field of **ethics**, Deleuze & Guattari have inspired significant contributions from Todd May, Simon O'Sullivan, Charles Stivale and Rosi Braidotti, whose work links ethics and philosophy with feminist theory and practice. The work of three philosophers and cultural critics engaging the topic of **religion**, William Connolly, Philip Goodchild, and Kenneth Surin, is also clearly influenced by Deleuze & Guattari. Given that Deleuze & Guattari considered all their collaborative work to be basically political in orientation, their influence in the field of **political** theory is extensive. In addition to Brian Massumi, who has published several important books and edited collections—often spanning the aesthetic and the political—Paul Patton has published works that connect Deleuze & Guattari with mainstream Anglo-American political thought as well as extend their thinking to post-colonial and aboriginal issues. Julian Reid has introduced the thought of Deleuze & Guattari to the field of International Relations, and Nick Thoburn has written an important book on the relations between Deleuze and Marx. Edouard Glissant adapts several of Deleuze & Guattari's concepts for the Caribbean context, while Jon Beasley-Murray draws substantially on Deleuze & Guattari (particularly the concepts of habit and affect) in his important critique of the concept of hegemony in cultural studies, using case studies from Latin America. My book on *Nomad Citizenship* combines the project of nomadology from *A Thousand Plateaus* with the utopian aspect of political philosophy made explicit in *What is Philosophy?* Hakim Bey's theory of the *Temporary Autonomous Zone* owes a great deal to Deleuze & Guattari, as does the massively popular trilogy by Michael Hardt and Toni Negri, *Empire*, *Multitude*, and *Commonwealth* (particularly the first two volumes). Hardt & Negri's concepts of Empire and Multitude are clearly related to Deleuze & Guattari's analysis of the global-capitalist war-machine and of machinic assemblages as rhizomatic multiplicities, respectively. Nevertheless it must be said that Hardt & Negri part company with Deleuze & Guattari regarding the question of history: where the latter consistently treat history as secondary to becomings, the former adopt a more familiar Hegelian-Marxist view of history that is both dialectical and teleological.

On the lasting significance of *A Thousand Plateaus*

In an oft-quoted remark (from "Theatrum Philosophicum," p. 165), Foucault suggested that "perhaps one day this [the 20th] century will be known as Deleuzian." According to a rejoinder almost as common as citations of Foucault's comment, it may be the 21st century rather than the 20th that becomes known as Deleuzian. Compared to Derrida—both "philosophers of difference" published their first important books in 1968–9—Deleuze & Guattari's influence was slow in coming, yet it appears likely to last longer than Derrida's, which in tandem with Foucault it has already eclipsed. Both Derrida and Deleuze & Guattari first gained entry into the English-speaking academy through the portal of literary studies, but while Derrida saw himself (following Heidegger) as bringing a long phase of western metaphysics to an end, Deleuze considered himself to be continuing and renewing a philosophical tradition stretching back to the ancient Greeks—although he did so more often than not by choosing maverick philosophers or paths less traveled within that tradition, as I suggested at the outset. Yet for Deleuze, re-reading and renewing even major philosophers such as Plato and Kant was equally important as bringing to light unjustly neglected philosophers such as Spinoza, Nietzsche and Bergson. The creation of concepts would remain the task of philosophy, which must continue to play a vital role in society by combatting orthodox common sense and formulating new possibilities of life, in fruitful collaboration with the sciences and the arts. The other distinctive difference between Deleuze and Derrida is the latter's textualism or linguo-centrism, inherited from structuralism. Derrida was a brilliant reader of texts (philosophical, literary, linguistic—texts of all kinds), but this made it difficult for him (early in his career, at least) to convincingly address issues outside the text. ("There is nothing outside the text," he was translated as saying.) Deleuze and Guattari were never as text-centric as Derrida. Indeed, in their first collaboration they take Lacanianism to task precisely for its linguo-centrism, and especially for structuring the unconscious as a language when it really operates more like a machine. Their critique of linguistics in *A Thousand Plateaus*, as we have seen, proceeds by immediately placing language in relation to its outside: the force of power and the continual transmogrification of the chaosmos. And, as we have also seen, the book draws substantially on a wide range of disciplines, and makes important interventions in many more. Ironically enough, the book that purports to be philosophy and nothing but philosophy nonetheless maintains contact with innumerable fields outside of philosophy itself—which can only enhance its prospects for lasting influence.

Another way of understanding the impact of *A Thousand Plateaus*, especially starting in the Anglophone academy, is to locate it at the intersection of two important fields, both of them inherently interdisciplinary, and both of which emerged in the last quarter of the last century when Deleuze and Guattari started collaborating: cultural studies and theory. Cultural studies developed principally out of intense dissatisfaction with the disciplinary limitations of literary studies, history and anthropology, and became interdisciplinary (if not anti-disciplinary) as a result. More importantly, the animus inspiring cultural studies was directed largely against the disciplines' inability to address pressing social problems such as unbridled militarism, rampant poverty in the midst of vast wealth, environmental catastrophe, unresponsive representative democracy, and so on. Cultural studies would draw on tools from whichever disciplines could be found useful to address problems that did not arise within (or were indeed excluded from) the purview of any one of them, and would produce "local knowledge" of immediate use in addressing such problems rather than contribute to the edifices of purportedly universal disciplinary knowledge. Its stance and *modus operandi* were therefore very similar to those Deleuze & Guattari described in *A Thousand Plateaus* as nomad or minor science. At the same time, the book itself was an astounding and outstanding example of what became known as "theory"—the practice, which had already started with structuralism, of drawing on a range of disparate fields (linguistics, anthropology, philosophy, economics, et al.) in order to produce novel research paradigms or strategies that didn't belong exclusively to any one of them, and which were then fed back into research projects in all these disciplines and more. *A Thousand Plateaus* simultaneously exemplified, encouraged, and enabled this kind of theoretical practice and theory-informed research—first in the humanities (especially literary and cultural studies), then the arts (especially architecture and music), and eventually the social sciences (especially geography and political theory).

Deleuze & Guattari's contributions can thus be considered "post-structuralist" in two senses of the term (even though the term would have meant little to them, or anyone else, in the French context). They were post-**structuralist** in the sense of extending the trans-disciplinary reach of theory, in continuity with the course already laid out by structuralism; yet they were **post**-structuralist in the sense of rescuing theory and theory-informed research from the very "linguistic turn" for which structuralism had been primarily responsible, and putting them back in touch with pressing problems in the outside world. The sheer range and number of titles in the "Deleuze Encounters" series published by Bloomsbury Academic and the "Deleuze Connections" and "New Directions in Deleuze Studies" series edited by Ian Buchanan and Claire Colebrook at Edinburgh University Press (*Deleuze and Space*, *Deleuze and Feminist Theory*, *Deleuze and Music*, and so forth) is eloquent testimony to the extent of Deleuze & Guattari's reach in "post-linguistic" research. But so are their contributions to a number of emerging fields in the humanities, arts, and social sciences, including what's called the "affective turn;" renewed interest in the body, space and architecture; "post-humanism;" the "new materialism;" and the alter-globalization movement, among others.

Even more distinctive of the trans-disciplinary reach of Deleuze & Guattari's work, however, is the unique opportunity it affords for enabling constructive dialogue between the "two cultures"—that is to say, between the hard sciences and mathematics, on one hand, and the arts and humanities and social sciences, on the other. As a species of "science fiction," as we have seen, *A Thousand Plateaus* draws extensively on **both** science and literature, on Darwin and Reimann as well as Kafka and Proust. In treating complexity theory and free indirect discourse with equal seriousness, Deleuze & Guattari end up constructing what I am tempted to call a unified field theory of the chaosmos as an open dynamic system, with philosophy as one of its mapping technologies, operating alongside of and inter-connecting with science and math and political anthropology and literature and the arts. To the extent that this is so, *A Thousand Plateaus* will have fulfilled its promise to provide the metaphysics appropriate to the sciences of today, and will become as influential in this and succeeding centuries as Kant's metaphysics has been from the time of the Enlightenment up until now.

CHAPTER FIVE

Further Reading

A selection of works by each of the authors listed below appears in the Bibliography.

Journals that have frequently featured work on Deleuze & Guattari in general include *Chimères*, *Futur Antérieur*, and *Multitudes* (online) in French; *Angelaki*, *Rhizomes* (online), *Substance*, and of course *Deleuze Studies*, in English. Key academic presses for scholarship on their work include Columbia, Continuum, Duke, Minnesota, Palgrave, Routledge, Zone Books—and especially the many topical volumes (too numerous to list) in the "Deleuze Encounters" series at Bloomsbury Academic and the two series at the Edinburgh University Press: "Deleuze Connections" and "Plateaus—New Directions in Deleuze Studies."

Other relevant works by Deleuze and Guattari

Among works by Deleuze and Guattari themselves, *Anti-Oedipus* is the obvious recommendation, it being the first volume of *Capitalism and Schizophrenia*, of which *A Thousand Plateaus* is the second. Their book on *Kafka*, published between the two volumes, is the other obvious choice, inasmuch as it constitutes both a fitting conclusion to the first volume, as an anti-oedipal reading of Kafka, and an equally fitting introduction to the second volume, as an introduction to the rhizome and micropolitics. Their final collaboration, *What is Philosophy?*, constitutes in many ways the best introduction to the philosophy they were doing in *A Thousand Plateaus*, as I have said. Among their single-author writings, Deleuze's *Proust and Signs* (particularly the 3rd edition) and Guattari's "Machine and Structure" (found in *Molecular Revolution*) are the most relevant, although they are both difficult. Deleuze's *Foucault* is more straightforward, and presents a conceptual apparatus similar to that of *A Thousand Plateaus*, although it was written later (1986). More generally, *Dialogues* and *Negotiations*, consisting of interviews and shorter essays, provide the easiest access to Deleuze's thought.

Expository works on Deleuze and Guattari in general

The English translator Brian Massumi's book, *user's guide to capitalism and schizophrenia*, is the obvious place to start; despite its general title, it mostly references *A Thousand Plateaus*, and hardly mentions the first volume at all. Even better is his "Preface" to the Chinese translation of the second volume, which lucidly and succinctly describes the process of concept-creation at work throughout *A Thousand Plateaus*. John Protevi and Mark Bonta's *Deleuze and Geophilosophy* provides an excellent overview of "Deleuzoguattarian geophilosophy" and an explanatory glossary of the terms used in *A Thousand Plateaus*, followed by a case study of how to do geography following Deleuze and Guattari.

For expository accounts of Deleuze & Guattari's collaborations prior to *A Thousand Plateaus*, see my *Deleuze & Guattari's Anti-Oedipus: Introduction to Schizoanalysis*, which thoroughly explicates their first collaboration and its relations to Freud, Marx, and Nietzsche (among others); and Gregg Lambert's *In Search of a New Image of Thought*, which shows what Proust and Kafka contribute to Deleuze & Guattari's conception of the image of thought. The best general introductions to Deleuze & Guattari's collaborative work are Ronald Bogue's *Deleuze and Guattari* and Philip Goodchild's, *Deleuze and Guattari: an Introduction to the Politics of Desire*. Gary Genosko compiled an exhaustive three-volume account of the reception of work by Deleuze (vol. 1), Guattari (vol. 2), and Deleuze & Guattari (vol. 3), entitled *Deleuze and Guattari: Critical Assessments of Leading Philosophers*, in 2001, but of course some of the best and most helpful work on Deleuze & Guattari has appeared since then. The best expository accounts of Guattari are Genosko's *Critical Introduction* and Janell Watson's *Guattari's Diagrammatic Thought*. The best expositions of Deleuze's philosophy include Eric Alliez's *Signature of the World*, Claire Colebrook's *Gilles Deleuze*, Michael Hardt's *Gilles Deleuze* (focused exclusively on his relations with Spinoza, Nietzsche and Bergson), Jean-Clet Martin's *Variations*, John Rajchman's *Deleuze Connections*, Daniel W. Smith's extensive collection of *Essays on Deleuze*, and a set of lucid and thorough books by James Williams, each devoted to one of Deleuze's important books or concepts. Ronald Bogue's three-volume examination of Deleuze & Guattari's approaches to literature, to cinema, and to music, painting and the arts are both thorough and accessible. The most comprehensive and succinct treatment of Deleuze's entire philosophical project, from his early work on Hume through the cinema books, is Joe Hughes' *Philosophy After Deleuze*. More advanced treatments of various aspects of Deleuze's philosophy include books by Brent Adkins, Ian Buchanan, Miguel de Beistegui, and Eleanor Kaufman.

There are several very good lexical guides to Deleuze & Guattari, found in Bonta & Protevi's *Deleuze and Geophilosophy*, Claire Colebrook's *Understanding Deleuze*, Adrian Parr's *Deleuze Dictionary*, Charles Stivale's *Gilles Deleuze: Key Concepts*, and François Zourabichvili's *The Vocabulary of Deleuze*.

The following suggestions for further reading are listed according to the topics of the preceding chapters and chapter sections. In his *Philosophy After Deleuze*, Joe Hughes divides Deleuze's philosophy into categories similar to the sections of Chapter Three, but orders them differently (style, ontology, ethics, aesthetics, and politics); in Part Two of his *Essays on Deleuze*, Daniel W. Smith instead categorizes Deleuze's philosophical system in strictly Kantian terms: aesthetics, dialectics, analytics, ethics, and politics.

Chapter 1 *A Thousand Plateaus* in context

François Dosse has written the best intellectual twin-biography of Deleuze & Guattari, including an interesting account of their collaboration. *The Anti-Oedipus Papers* details the collaborative writing process for the first volume, mostly from the perspective of Guattari. Jones and Roffe's collection, *Deleuze's Philosophical Lineage*, meanwhile, provides insights into all the important philosophers on whom Deleuze drew in developing his own philosophical perspective.

On Deleuze's pre-psychoanalytic, philosophical understanding of the unconscious, see his book on Hume, his introductory essay on "Instincts and Institutions," Jeffrey Bell's *Deleuze's Hume*, my essay on "Deleuze and Psychoanalysis," and Christian Kerslake's book on *Deleuze and the Unconscious*.

On Deleuze's relation to Kant, see of course his book on *Kant's Critical Philosophy*; several of Daniel W. Smith's *Essays on Deleuze*; Joe Hughes' *Philosophy After Deleuze*; Christian Kerslake's *Immanence and the Vertigo of Philosophy*; Alberto Toscano's *The Theater of Production*; and Willat and Lee's collection, *Thinking between Deleuze and Kant*.

On the relations between Christianity and capitalism, see William Connolly's book on *Capitalism and Christianity, American style*.

For more on jazz improvisation as an example of de-territorialization, see my essay on "Jazz Improvisation," and on the relations between improvising and market behaviors, see my essay on "Affirmative Nomadology."

For a more detailed account of the image of thought in Proust and Kafka, see Gregg Lambert's book, *In Search of a New Image of Thought*.

On the relations between science and philosophy and the virtual and the actual, see my *Nomad Citizenship*, especially Chapter 1; and the essays collected in Peter Gaffney's *The Force of the Virtual*.

Chapter 2 Overview of themes

For more on Deleuze's complex philosophy of time, see his *Difference and Repetition*, especially Chapter Two; James Williams'

Gilles Deleuze's Philosophy of Time; Jay Lampert's *Deleuze and Guattari's Philosophy of History*; Craig Lundy's *History and Becoming*; and my essay on "Non-linear Historical Materialism." Elizabeth Grosz links Deleuze's philosophy of time to those of Darwin, Nietzsche and Bergson in her book, *The Nick of Time* and explores its implications for politics in *Time Travels*.

On the concept of a chaosmos, see Guattari's *Chaosmosis*.

For more on the relations between the virtual and the actual couched in complexity theory terms, see Manuel DeLanda's *Intensive Science & Virtual Philosophy*; Bonta and Protevi's *Deleuze and Geophilosophy*; and Jeffrey Bell's *Philosophy at the Edge of Chaos*. For more on the paradigm of self-organization, see Stuart Kauffman's *At Home in the Universe*.

On the three libidinal modes of production, see in addition to *Anti-Oedipus* itself my *Introduction to Schizoanalysis*.

On the utopian vocation of philosophical concept-creation in the context of contemporary capitalist society, marketing, and massified public opinion, see *What is Philosophy?* and my *Nomad Citizenship*, Chapter 1.

Chapter 3 Reading the text

Epistemology

On complexity theory and terms such as basins of attraction, see works by Bonta & Protevi, Manuel DeLanda, Prigogine & Stengers, and Stuart Kauffman.

For more detailed discussion of the process of concept-creation, see Deleuze & Guattari's *What is Philosophy?*, Massumi's "Preface," and Chapter 1 of my *Nomad Citizenship*.

On the importance of Events in Deleuze, see Zourabichvili.

On the notion of "reciprocal presupposition," see Louis Hjelmslev's *Prolegomena*.

For extended discussions of the image of thought, see Lambert's *In Search of a New Image of Thought* and Gregory Flaxman's *Fabulation of Philosophy*.

On the importance of overturning Platonism to Deleuze, see his essay on "Plato and the Simulacrum."

For an extended discussion of the distinction between strategy and tactics, see de Certeau.

The exchange between Deleuze and Foucault regarding theory and practice is to be found in "Intellectuals and Power."

On the history of modern science and its forms of thought, see Isabelle Stengers' *The Invention of Modern Science* and Gregory Flaxman's *Fabulation of Philosophy*; see also more generally the essays collected in John Marks' *Deleuze and Science*.

For an extended discussion of movement and speed in Deleuze & Guattari's thought, see Brian Massumi's *Parables for the Virtual*.

For a more extensive discussion of nomad science and its relation to jazz, see my *Nomad Citizenship*.

On the unpredictability of fluid dynamics, see Deleuze's essay on "Lucretius and the Simulacrum" and Michel Serres' *Birth of Physics*.

The distinction between *bricolage* and engineering is developed by Lévi-Strauss in *The Savage Mind*.

We owe the most extensive critique of hylomorphism to the (untranslated) work of French philosopher Gilbert Simondon; in addition to Bonta & Protevi's glossary entry, see the essays collected by De Boever in *Gilbert Simondon* and Muriel Combes' *Gilbert Simondon and the Philosophy of the Transindividual*.

Onto-aesthetics

For more on the concept of expression in Deleuze, see his *Expressionism in Philosophy* and Lambert's *In Search of a New Image of Thought*.

On the relations between art and nature, see Elizabeth Grosz, *Chaos, Territory, Art* and *Becoming Undone*.

Bonta & Protevi and DeLanda make extensive use of the concept of stratification; see the latter's *A Thousand Years of Non-linear History* and his (unfortunately misnamed) *A New Philosophy of Society*.

Foucault analyzes the prison-delinquency complex in his *Discipline and Punish*; see also Deleuze's book on *Foucault*.

For more on the molar/molecular relation, see Bonta & Protevi's *Geophilosophy* and Stengers' *Invention of Modern Science*.

On the relations between refrain and territory, see Ronald Bogue's essay, "Minority, Territory, Music."

In *Without Criteria*, Steven Shaviro examines Deleuze's aesthetics in relation to Kant and Whitehead; and in *Blake, Deleuzian Aesthetics and the Digital*, Claire Colebrook develops a Deleuzian aesthetics to link Blake with the present.

On aesthetics more generally, see Stephen Zepke's *Art as Abstract Machine*; Simon O'Sullivan's *Art Encounters Deleuze and Guattari*; and the essays collected by Brian Massumi in *A Shock to Thought*; by Marcel Swiboda in *Deleuze and Music*; by O'Sullivan and Zepke in *Deleuze, Guattari and the Production of the New*; by Hulse and Nesbitt in *Sounding the Virtual*, and by Zepke and O'Sullivan in *Deleuze and Contemporary Art*.

Anthro-ethology

For relevant background on linguistics and philosophy of language, see J. L. Austin's *How to Do Things With Words*, V. N. Voloshinov's *Marxism and the Philosophy of Language*, and Louis Hjelmslev's *Prolegomena*. For more on Deleuze's philosophy of language, see Jean-Jacques Lecercle's *Deleuze and Language*.

On money originating in debt payments rather than trade, see David Graeber's book on *Debt*.

For more on *potlatch*, see Marcel Mauss, *The Gift and Potlatch*, and on a-cephalous societies, see Pierre Clastres, *Society Against the State*.

On mega-machines, see Lewis Mumford, *The Myth of the Machine*, especially Volume One.

Ethics

Todd May's *Gilles Deleuze* provides an excellent introduction to the ethics of Deleuzian thought, after which *Deleuze and Guattari's Immanent Ethics* by Tamsin Lorraine provides a fuller development. More advanced treatment of ethical issues is found in several of Daniel W. Smith's *Essays on Deleuze* and in Simon O'Sullivan's *On the Production of Subjectivity*. The ethics of friendship is central to

Charles Stivale's *Gilles Deleuze's ABCs*. Much of Rosi Braidotti's ground-breaking work operates at the intersection of ethics and politics. Similarly, Ronald Bogue's essays in *Deleuze's Way* operate at the intersection of ethics and aesthetics. The essays by Gregory Seigworth and J. Macgregor Wise in *Animations of Deleuze and Guattari* demonstrate how the concept of the refrain illuminates ethical issues in everyday life and professional life. See also the essays collected by Jun and Smith in *Deleuze and Ethics* and by Elizabeth Grosz in *Becomings*.

On the concept of the Body-without-Organs, see *Anti-Oedipus*, of course, and my *Introduction to Schizoanalysis*. On the BwO as locus of self-transformation, see Paul Patton's discussion of "critical freedom" in *Deleuze and the Political* (pp. 83–7).

On multiplicities, see Deleuze's book on *Bergsonism* and his important essays, "Bergson" and "Bergson's Conception of Difference."

For a Deleuzian examination of sex, see Frida Beckman's *Between Desire and Pleasure* and the collection she edited, *Deleuze and Sex*.

On the distinction between forms of power, see Canetti's *Crowds and Power*; and for more on his analysis of the symphony orchestra conductor as a model of power, see my essay on "Jazz Improvisation."

For more on Deleuze and literature, see his *Coldness and Cruelty*, *Proust and Signs*, *Essays Critical and Clinical*; Ronald Bogue's *Deleuzian Fabulation*; Jean-Jacques Lecercle's *Badiou and Deleuze Read Literature*; Aidan Tynan's *Deleuze's Literary Clinic*; and the essays collected by Buchanan and Marks in *Deleuze and Literature*.

On becoming-woman, Deleuze and feminism, see in addition to Alice Jardine's "Women in Limbo;" Rosi Braidotti's *Nomadic Subjects*, *Nomadic Theory*, *Transpositions: on Nomadic Ethics*, and *Metamorphoses*; Elizabeth Grosz's *Volatile Bodies*; and Tamsin Lorraine's *Irigaray and Deleuze*; see also the essays collected by Buchanan and Colebrook in *Deleuze and Feminist Theory* and by Nigianni and Storr in *Deleuze and Queer Theory*.

On issues surrounding the concept of becoming-minoritarian, see the essays collected by Saldanha and Adams in *Deleuze and Race*.

Politics

For an introductory overview, see Paul Patton's essay on "The Political Philosophy of Deleuze and Guattari." Important books influenced by aspects of Deleuze & Guattari's thought include Jon Beasley-Murray's *Posthegemony*; Elizabeth Grosz's *Becoming Undone*, *The Nick of Time* and *Space, Time and Perversion*; Hardt & Negri's *Empire*, *Multitude*, and *Commonwealth*; my *Nomad Citizenship*; Brian Massumi's *The Politics of Everyday Fear* and *Semblance and Event*; Thomas Nail's *Returning to Revolution*; Davide Panagia's *The Poetics of Political Thinking* and *The Political Life of Sensation*; Adrian Parr's *Deleuze and Memorial Culture* and *The Wrath of Capital*; Paul Patton's *Deleuze and the Political* and *Deleuzian Concepts*; Nick Thoburn's *Deleuze, Marx and Politics*; and Nathan Widders' *Reflections on Time and Politics* and *Political Theory after Deleuze*. See also the essays collected by Thoburn and Buchanan in *Deleuze and Politics*, by Bignall and Patton in *Deleuze and the Postcolonial*, by Fuglsang and Sørensen in *Deleuze and the Social*, and by Buchanan and Parr in *Deleuze and the Contemporary World*.

On the standard notion of segmentarity in political anthropology, see Georges Balandier's *Political Anthropology*.

For the sociology of Gabriel Tarde, see his *Laws of Imitation* and a selection of his writings, *Gabriel Tarde on Communication and Social Influence*.

On the concept of "microfacism," see John Protevi's "A Problem of Pure Matter" and my "Schizoanalysis, Nomadology, Fascism."

For more on nomadism and nomadology, see my *Nomad Citizenship*, and for the war-machine, see my "Affirmative Nomadology and the War Machine."

For an account of Deleuze & Guattari's Marxism, see my essay on "Karl Marx" in Jones and Roffe's *Deleuze's Philosophical Lineage* and my *Nomad Citizenship*, especially Chapter 4.

On the oscillation between the bond and the pact forms of the State under contemporary capitalism, see my *Nomad Citizenship*, especially Chapter 2.

NOTES

Chapter One

1 Edmund Husserl was a twentieth-century mathematician and philosopher, and a founder of phenomenology; Martin Heidegger, a student of Husserl, developed a philosophy of existential phenomenology.
2 Baruch Spinoza was an early-modern Jewish-Dutch philosopher; Friedrich Nietzsche was a late nineteenth-century materialist philosopher; Henri Bergson was an early twentieth-century French philosopher.
3 Gottfried Wilhelm Leibniz was a late seventeenth-century German philosopher and mathematician, one of the founders of calculus; David Hume was an eighteenth-century Scottish empiricist philosopher; Carl Jung was an early twentieth-century psychiatrist, second only to Freud as a founder of psychoanalysis; Louis Hjelmslev was a twentieth-century Danish linguist responsible for further developing several of Saussure's important concepts.
4 Although the appropriateness of the Copernican analogy is the subject of considerable debate, Kant did insist that reliable knowledge of objects would have to be correlated with the faculties that human subjects use to produce knowledge, rather than directly with properties inherent in the objects themselves.

Chapter Two

1 This is what Deleuze said, in a course he gave at Vincennes in October 1987: "Il faut faire la métaphysique qui est le corrélat de la science moderne, exactement comme la science moderne est le corrélat d'une métaphysique potentielle qu'on a pas encore su faire." Cours Vincennes – St Denis : l évènement, Whitehead – 10/03/1987 – http://www.webdeleuze.com/php/texte.php?cle=140&groupe=Leibniz&langue=1 (Accessed 11/28/2012).

2 See Jay Lampert's *Deleuze and Guattari's Philosophy of History* for this characterization.

Chapter Three

1 Technically, there is a fifteenth plateau following "The Smooth and the Striated," but it functions as a kind of annotated index to some of the book's key terms, and doesn't add anything new—so I leave it out of my account in what follows.
2 Taylorization refers to the process developed by turn of the nineteenth-twentieth-century business management consultant Frederick Winslow Taylor, whereby the movements and activities of each factory worker were dissected into their smallest parts which were then re-combined in order to maximize speed and efficiency. With Taylorization, the workplace becomes a thoroughly striated space.
3 Bernhard Reimann was a ground-breaking nineteenth-century German mathematician, one of whose innovations was to use more than three or four dimensions to model physical reality; Reimannian geometry became an important alternative to conventional Euclidean geometry, and provided a basis for Einstein's theory of relativity.
4 Inexplicably, Massumi translates "esprits libres" as "free spirits," when the more accurate translation is "free minds," particularly given the context (which is philosophical) and the misleading connotations in English of "free spirits" (referring to persons prone to unrestrained behavior).
5 Søren Kierkegaarde: nineteenth-century Danish philosopher, theologian, poet, and social critic; Friedrich Nietzsche: nineteenth-century German philosopher, poet, cultural critic, and classical philologist; Antonin Artaud: early twentieth-century French playwright, poet, actor and theatre director who spent years of his life in sanatoriums; Heinrich von Kleist: turn-of-the-eighteenth-nineteenth-century German poet, dramatist, novelist and short story writer whose life ended in the murder-suicide of his lover and himself; Maurice Blanchot: twentieth-century French writer, philosopher, and literary theorist whose intellectual outlook was akin to those of Deleuze, Derrida, and Foucault.
6 The Great Chain of Being refers to a religious conception of the cosmos derived from Plato and Aristotle whereby all beings are linked in a strict hierarchical order with a deity at the apex.

7 The Stoics were a group of influential ancient Greek philosophers who advocated self-control and fortitude (rather than resignation), and whose doctrines remained influential up through the Roman Empire.

8 Following Spinoza, Deleuze & Guattari distinguish categorically between *pouvoir* and *puissance*, often translated as power and force. *Pouvoir* designates a **limiting** power wielded **over** others, whereas *puissance* designates an **enhanced** strength arising from cooperation **with** others.

9 See Deleuze's important essay "Postscript on Control Societies."

Chapter Four

1 I leave aside the critical responses by Fredric Jameson, Slavoj Žižek, and Alain Badiou, since they all bear exclusively on works preceding *A Thousand Plateaus*. For accounts of their reception of Deleuze & Guattari, see Lambert (2006) for the first two; and for the third, see Roffe (2012). See also Daniel W. Smith's "Badiou and Deleuze on the ontology of mathematics," "Mathematics and the Theory of Multiplicities: Deleuze and Badiou Revisited," and "The Inverse Side of the Structure: Žižek on Deleuze on Lacan."

BIBLIOGRAPHY

Adkins, B. (2007) *Death and Desire in Hegel, Heidegger and Deleuze*, Edinburgh: Edinburgh University Press.
Alliez, E. (2004) *The Signature of the World, or, What is Deleuze and Guattari's Philosophy?*, New York and London: Continuum.
Althusser, L. (2006) *Philosophy of the Encounter: Later Writings, 1978–87*, London and New York: Verso.
Attali, J. (1985) *Noise: the Political Economy of Music*, Minneapolis: University of Minnesota Press.
Austin, J. L. (1962) *How to Do Things with Words*, Cambridge, MA: Harvard University Press.
Balandier, G. (1970) *Political Anthropology*, New York: Pantheon Books.
Ballantyne, A. (2007) *Deleuze and Guattari for Architects*, London and New York: Routledge.
Beasley-Murray, J. (2011) *Posthegemony*, Minneapolis: University of Minnesota Press.
Beckman, F. (2013) *Between Desire and Pleasure: A Deleuzian Theory of Sexuality*, Edinburgh: Edinburgh University Press.
—(ed.) (2011) *Deleuze and Sex*, Edinburgh: Edinburgh University Press.
Bell, J. (2006) *Philosophy at the Edge of Chaos: Gilles Deleuze and the Philosophy of Difference*, Toronto; Buffalo: University of Toronto Press.
—(2009) *Deleuze's Hume: Philosophy, Culture and the Scottish Enlightenment*, Edinburgh: Edinburgh University Press.
Bey, H. (2003) *T.A.Z.: the Temporary Autonomous Zone, Ontological Anarchy, Poetic Terrorism*, Brooklyn, NY: Autonomedia.
Bignall, S. and P. Patton (eds) (2010) *Deleuze and the Postcolonial*, Edinburgh: Edinburgh University Press.
Bogue, R. (1989) *Deleuze and Guattari*, New York and London: Routledge.
—(2003a) *Deleuze on Cinema*, New York and London: Routledge.
—(2003b) *Deleuze on Literature*, New York and London: Routledge.
—(2003c) *Deleuze on Music, Painting, and the Arts*, New York and London: Routledge.
—(2003d) "Minority, Territory, Music", in J. Khalfa (ed.) *Introduction to the Philosophy of Gilles Deleuze*, Continuum, pp. 114–32.

—(2007) *Deleuze's Way: Essays in Transverse Ethics and Aesthetics*, Aldershot, England; Burlington, VT: Ashgate.
—(2010) *Deleuzian Fabulation and the Scars of History*, Edinburgh University Press.
Bonta, M. and J. Protevi (2004) *Deleuze and Geophilosophy: a Guide and Glossary*, Edinburgh: Edinburgh University Press.
Boundas, C. (ed.) (1993) *The Deleuze Reader*, New York: Columbia University Press.
—(2006) *Deleuze and Philosophy*, Edinburgh: Edinburgh University Press.
—(2009) *Gilles Deleuze: the Intensive Reduction*, London and New York: Continuum.
Boundas, C. and Dorothea Olkowski (eds) (1994) *Gilles Deleuze and the Theater of Philosophy*, New York: Routledge.
Braidotti, R. (2002) *Metamorphoses: Towards a Materialist Theory of Becoming*, Cambridge: Polity; Malden, MA: Blackwell.
—(2006) *Transpositions: on Nomadic Ethics*, Cambridge and Malden, MA: Polity Press.
—(2011a) *Nomadic Subjects: Embodiment and Sexual Difference in Contemporary Feminist Theory*, New York: Columbia University Press.
—(2011b) *Nomadic Theory: the Portable Rosi Braidotti*, New York: Columbia University Press.
Brott, S. (2011) *Architecture for a Free Subjectivity: Deleuze and Guattari at the Horizon of the Real*, Farnham, Surrey and Burlington, VT: Ashgate.
Buchanan, I. (2000) *Deleuzism: a Metacommentary*, Durham, North Carolina: Duke University Press.
Buchanan, I. and C. Colebrook (eds) (2000) *Deleuze and Feminist Theory*, Edinburgh: Edinburgh University Press.
Buchanan, I. and J. Marks (eds) (2000) *Deleuze and Literature*, Edinburgh: Edinburgh University Press.
Buchanan, I. and A. Parr (eds) (2006) *Deleuze and the Contemporary World*, Edinburgh: Edinburgh University Press.
Buchanan, I. and M. Swiboda (eds) (2006) *Deleuze and Music*, Edinburgh: Edinburgh University Press.
Canetti, E. (1966) *Crowds and Power*, New York: Viking Press.
Clastres, P. (1989) *Society against the State: Essays in Political Anthropology*, New York: Zone Books; Cambridge, MA: MIT Press.
Colebrook, C. (2002) *Understanding Deleuze*, Crows Nest: Allen & Unwin.
—(2012) *Blake, Deleuzian Aesthetics and the Digital*, London and New York: Continuum.

Colebrook, C. and J. Weinstein (eds) (2008) *Deleuze and Gender*, Edinburgh: Edinburgh University Press.
Combes, M. (2013) *Gilbert Simondon and the Philosophy of the Transindividual*, Cambridge, MA: MIT Press.
Connolly, W. E. (2002) *Neuropolitics: Thinking, Culture, Speed*, Minneapolis: University of Minnesota Press.
—(2008) *Capitalism and Christianity, American Style*, Durham, North Carolina: Duke University Press.
—(2011) *A World of Becoming*, Durham, North Carolina: Duke University Press.
De Beistegui, M. (2010) *Immanence: Deleuze and Philosophy*, Edinburgh: Edinburgh University Press.
De Boever, A. et al. (eds) (2012) *Gilbert Simondon: Being and Technology*, Edinburgh: Edinburgh University Press.
De Certeau, M. (1984) *The Practice of Everyday Life*, Vol. 1, Berkeley: University of California Press.
DeLanda, M. (1997) *A Thousand Years of Nonlinear History*, New York: Zone Books.
—(2002) *Intensive Science and Virtual Philosophy*, London and New York: Continuum.
—(2006) *A New Philosophy of Society: Assemblage Theory and Social Complexity*, London and New York: Continuum.
Deleuze, G. (1984) *Kant's Critical Philosophy: the Doctrine of the Faculties*, Minneapolis: University of Minnesota Press.
—(1988) *Foucault*, Minneapolis: University of Minnesota Press.
—(1990a) *Expressionism in Philosophy: Spinoza*, New York: Zone Books.
—(1990b) *The Logic of Sense*, New York: Columbia University Press.
—(1990c) "Plato and the Simulacrum", in *The Logic of Sense*, pp. 253–66.
—(1990d) 'Lucretius and the Simulacrum', in *The Logic of Sense*, pp. 266–79.
—(1991a) *Bergsonism*, New York: Zone Books.
—(1991b) *Empiricism and Subjectivity: an Essay on Hume's Theory of Human Nature*, New York: Columbia University Press.
—(1991c) *Masochism: Coldness and Cruelty*, New York: Zone Books; Cambridge, MA: MIT Press.
—(1993) *The Fold: Leibniz and the Baroque*, Minneapolis: University of Minnesota Press.
—1994) *Difference and Repetition*, New York: Columbia University Press.
—(1995a) *Negotiations 1972–1990*, New York: Columbia University Press.

—(1995b) "Postscript on Control Societies", in *Negotiations*, pp. 177–82.
—(1997) *Essays Critical and Clinical*, Minneapolis: University of Minnesota Press.
—(2000) *Proust and Signs*, Minneapolis: University of Minnesota Press.
—(2001) *Pure Immanence: Essays on a Life*, New York: Zone Books.
—(2002) *Dialogues II*, London and New York: Continuum.
—(2004a) *Desert Islands and Other Texts, 1953–1974*, New York: Semiotext(e).
—(2004b) "Instincts and Institutions", in *Desert Islands*, pp. 19–21.
—(2004c) "Bergson, 1859–1941", in *Desert Islands*, pp. 22–31.
—(2004d) "Bergson's Conception of Difference", in *Desert Islands*, pp. 32–51.
—(2006) *Nietzsche and Philosophy*, New York: Columbia University Press.
Deleuze, G. and M. Foucault (2004) "Intellectuals and Power", in *Desert Islands and Other Texts, 1953–1974*, New York: Semiotext(e), pp. 206–13.
Deleuze, G. and F. Guattari (1976) *Rhizome: Introduction*, Paris: Editions de Minuit.
—(1980) *Capitalism and Schizophrenia, Vol. 1: Anti-Oedipus*, Minneapolis: University of Minnesota Press.
—(1986) *Kafka: Toward a Minor Literature*, Minneapolis: University of Minnesota Press.
—(1987) *Capitalism and Schizophrenia, Vol. 2: A Thousand Plateaus*, Minneapolis: University of Minnesota Press.
—(1994) *What is Philosophy?*, New York: Columbia University Press.
Deleuze, G. and C. Parnet (2002) *Dialogues*, New York: Columbia University Press.
Dosse, F. (2010) *Gilles Deleuze & Félix Guattari: Intersecting Lives*, New York: Columbia University Press.
Flaxman, G. (2012) *Gilles Deleuze and the Fabulation of Philosophy*, Minneapolis: University of Minnesota Press.
Foucault, M. (1977) "Theatrum Philosophicum", in *Language, Countermemory, Practice*, Ithaca: Cornell University Press, pp. 165–98.
—(1995) *Discipline and Punish: the Birth of the Prison*, New York: Vintage Books.
Frichot, H. and S. Loo (eds) (2013) *Deleuze and Architecture*, Edinburgh: University Press.
Fuglsang, M. and B. M. Sørensen (eds) (2006) *Deleuze and the Social*, Edinburgh: Edinburgh University Press.
Gaffney, P. (ed.) (2010) *The Force of the Virtual: Deleuze, Science, and Philosophy*, Minneapolis: University of Minnesota Press.

Genosko, G. (2009) *Félix Guattari: a Critical Introduction*, London and New York: Pluto Press; New York: Palgrave Macmillan.

—(ed.) (2001) *Deleuze and Guattari: Critical Assessments of Leading Philosophers*, London and New York: Routledge, 3 vols: Vol. 1 – Deleuze; Vol. 2 – Guattari; Vol. 3 – Deleuze & Guattari.

Glissant, E. (1989) *Caribbean Discourse: Selected Essays*, Charlottesville: University Press of Virginia.

—(1997) *Poetics of Relation*, Ann Arbor: University of Michigan Press.

Goodchild, P. (1996a) *Deleuze and Guattari: an Introduction to the Politics of Desire*, London; Thousand Oaks, CA: Sage.

—(1996b) *Gilles Deleuze and the Question of Philosophy*, Madison: Fairleigh Dickinson University Press; London; Cranbury, NJ: Associated University Presses.

—(2002) *Capitalism and Religion: the Price of Piety*, London; New York: Routledge.

—(2009) *Theology of Money*, Durham: Duke University Press.

Graeber, D. (2011) *Debt: the First 5,000 Years*, Brooklyn, NY: Melville House.

Grossberg, L. (1991) "Rock, Territorialization and Power", *Cultural Studies*, 5:3, pp. 358–67.

—(1992) *We Gotta Get out of this Place: Popular Conservatism and Postmodern Culture*, New York: Routledge.

—(1993) 'Cultural studies and/in New Worlds', *Critical Studies in Mass Communication*, 10:1, pp. 1–22.

—(1997) "Cultural Studies, Modern Logics, and Theories of Globalisation", in *Back to Reality?: Social Experience and Cultural Studies*, A. McRobbie (ed.) Manchester University Press, pp. 7–35.

—(2003) "Animations, Articulations, and Becomings: An Introduction" in *Animations of Deleuze and Guattari*, J. D. Slack (ed.) New York: P. Lang, pp. 1–8.

—(2010) *Cultural Studies in the Future Tense*, Durham, North Carolina: Duke University Press.

Grosz, E. (1994) *Volatile Bodies: Toward a Corporeal Feminism*, Bloomington: Indiana University Press.

—(2001) *Architecture from the Outside: Essays on Virtual and Real Space*, foreword by Peter Eisenman, Cambridge, MA: MIT Press.

—(2004) *The Nick of Time: Politics, Evolution, and the Untimely*, Durham, North Carolina: Duke University Press.

—(2005) *Time Travels: Feminism, Nature, Power*, Durham, North Carolina: Duke University Press.

—(2008) *Chaos, Territory, Art: Deleuze and the Framing of the Earth*, New York: Columbia University Press.

—(2011) *Becoming undone: Darwinian Reflections on Life, Politics, and Art*, Durham, North Carolina: Duke University Press.
—(ed.) (1999) *Becomings: Explorations in Time, Memory, and Futures*, Ithaca, NY: Cornell University Press.
Guattari, F. (1984) *Molecular Revolution: Psychiatry and Politics*, Harmondsworth, Middlesex; New York: Penguin.
—(1995) *Chaosmosis: an Ethico-aesthetic Paradigm*, Bloomington, IN: Indiana University Press.
—(2000) *The Three Ecologies*, London; New Brunswick, NJ: Athlone Press.
—(2006) *The Anti-Oedipus Papers*, New York: Semiotext(e); Cambridge, MA: MIT Press.
Guattari, F. and A. Negri (1990) *Communists like Us: New Spaces of Liberty, New Lines of Alliance*, New York: Semiotext(e).
Hallward, P. (2006) *Out of this World: Deleuze and the Philosophy of Creation*, London and New York: Verso.
Haraway, D. (1991) "A Cyborg Manifesto: Science, Technology, and Socialist-Feminism in the Late Twentieth Century", in *Simians, Cyborgs, and Women: The Reinvention of Nature*, New York: Routledge, pp. 149–81.
Hardt, M. (1993) *Gilles Deleuze: an Apprenticeship in Philosophy*, Minneapolis: University of Minnesota Press.
Hardt, M. and A. Negri (2000) *Empire*, Cambridge, MA: Harvard University Press.
—(2004) *Multitude: War and Democracy in the Age of Empire*, New York: The Penguin Press.
—(2009) *Commonwealth*, Cambridge, MA: Harvard University Press.
Hjlemslev, L. (1969) *Prolegomena to a Theory of Language*, Madison: University of Wisconsin Press.
Holland, E. W. (1999) *Deleuze & Guattari's "Anti-Oedipus": Introduction to Schizoanalysis*, New York: Routledge.
—(2003) "Representation and Misrepresentation in Postcolonial Literature and Theory", *Research in African Literatures*, 34:1, pp. 159–73.
—(2008a) "Jazz Improvisation: Music of the People-to-Come", in *Deleuze, Guattari, and the Production of the New*, S. O'Sullivan and S. Zepke (eds) London: Continuum, pp. 196–205.
—(2008b) "Schizoanalysis, Nomadology, Fascism", in *Deleuze and Politics*, N. Thoburn and I. Buchanan (eds) Edinburgh: Edinburgh University Press, pp. 74–97.
—(2009a) "Affirmative Nomadology and the War Machine", in *Gilles Deleuze: the Intensive Reduction*, C. Boundas (ed.) London: Continuum, pp. 218–25.

—(2009b) "Karl Marx", in *Deleuze's Philosophical Lineage*, G. Jones and J. Roffe (eds) Edinburgh: Edinburgh University Press, pp. 147–66.
—(2012a) "Deleuze and Psychoanalysis", in *The Cambridge Companion to Gilles Deleuze*, D. W. Smith and H. Somers-Hall (eds) Cambridge: Cambridge University Press, pp. 307–36.
—(2012b) "Non-Linear Historical Materialism; Or, What is Revolutionary in Deleuze and Guattari's Philosophy of History?", in *Time and History in Deleuze and Serres*, B. Herzogenrath (ed.) London: Continuum, pp. 17–30.
Hughes, J. (2012) *Philosophy After Deleuze: Deleuze and the Genesis of Representation*, London and New York: Bloomsbury Academic.
Hulse, B. and N. Nesbitt (eds) (2010) *Sounding the Virtual: Gilles Deleuze and the Theory and Philosophy of Music*, Farnham, Surrey, England; Burlington, VT: Ashgate.
Jardine, A. (1984) "Woman in Limbo: Deleuze and his Br(others)," *SubStance* 13:3/4, pp. 46–60.
Jones, G. and J. Roffe (eds) (2009) *Deleuze's Philosophical Lineage*, Edinburgh: Edinburgh University Press.
Jun, N. and D. W. Smith (eds) (2011) *Deleuze and Ethics*, Edinburgh: Edinburgh University Press.
Karatani, K. (1995) *Architecture as Metaphor: Language, Number, Money*, Cambridge, MA: MIT Press.
Kauffman, S. (1995) *At Home in the Universe: the Search for Laws of Self-organization and Complexity*, New York: Oxford University Press.
Kaufman, E. (2012) *Deleuze, the Dark Precursor: Dialectic, Structure, Being*, Baltimore: The Johns Hopkins University Press.
Kerslake, C. (2007) *Deleuze and the Unconscious*, London and New York: Continuum.
—(2009) *Immanence and the Vertigo of Philosophy: from Kant to Deleuze*, Edinburgh: Edinburgh University Press.
Lambert, G. (2006) *Who's Afraid of Deleuze and Guattari?*, London and New York: Continuum.
—(2012) *In Search of a New Image of Thought: Gilles Deleuze and Philosophical Expressionism*, Minneapolis: University of Minnesota Press.
Latour, B. (1993) *We Have Never Been Modern*, Cambridge, MA: Harvard University Press.
Lecercle, J.-J. (2002) *Deleuze and language*, Houndmills, Basingstoke, Hampshire and New York: Palgrave Macmillan.
—(2010) *Badiou and Deleuze Read Literature*, Edinburgh: Edinburgh University Press.

Lévi-Strauss, C. (1966) *The Savage Mind*, Chicago: Chicago University Press.
Lévy, P. (1997) *Collective Intelligence: Mankind's Emerging World in Cyberspace*, Cambridge, MA: Perseus Books.
—(1998) *Becoming Virtual: Reality in the Digital Age*, New York: Plenum Trade.
—(2001) *Cyberculture*, Minneapolis, MN; London: University of Minnesota Press.
Lorraine, T. (1999) *Irigaray and Deleuze: Experiments in Visceral Philosophy*, Ithaca: Cornell University Press.
—(2011) *Deleuze and Guattari's Immanent Ethics: Theory, Subjectivity, and Duration*, Albany: State University of New York Press.
Lundy, C. (2012) *History and Becoming: Deleuze's Philosophy of Creativity*, Edinburgh: Edinburgh University Press.
Lyotard, J.-F. (1993) *Libidinal Economy*, Bloomington, IN: Indiana University Press.
Marks, J. (2006) *Deleuze and Science*, Edinburgh: Edinburgh University Press.
Martin, J.-C. (2010) *Variations: The Philosophy of Gilles Deleuze*, Edinburgh: Edinburgh University Press.
Massumi, B. (1992) *A user's guide to capitalism and schizophrenia: deviations from Deleuze and Guattari*, Cambridge, MA: MIT Press.
—(2002a) *Parables for the Virtual: Movement, Affect, Sensation*, Durham, North Carolina: Duke University Press.
—(2010) "What Concepts Do: Preface to the Chinese Translation of *A Thousand Plateaus*", *Deleuze Studies*, 4:1, pp. 1–15.
—(2011) *Semblance and Event: Activist Philosophy and the Occurrent Arts*, Cambridge, MA: MIT Press.
—(ed.) (1993) *The Politics of Everyday Fear*, Minneapolis: University of Minnesota Press.
—(ed.) (2002b) *A Shock to Thought: Expression after Deleuze and Guattari*, London and New York: Routledge.
Mauss, M. (2003) *The Gift and Potlatch*, London and New York: Routledge.
May, T. (2005) *Gilles Deleuze: an Introduction*, New York: Cambridge University Press.
Miller, C. (1998) *Nationalists and Nomads: Essays on Francophone African Literature and Culture*, Chicago: University of Chicago Press.
Mumford, L. (1967) *The Myth of the Machine*, New York: Harcourt, Brace & World.
Nail, T. (2012) *Returning to Revolution: Deleuze, Guattari and Zapatismo*, Edinburgh: Edinburgh University Press.

Nigianni, C. and Merl Storr (eds) (2009) *Deleuze and Queer Theory*, Edinburgh: Edinburgh University Press.
O'Sullivan, S. (2006) *Art Encounters Deleuze and Guattari: Thought beyond Representation*, Basingstoke; New York: Palgrave Macmillan.
—(2012) *On the Production of Subjectivity: Five Diagrams of the Finite-infinite Relation*, Houndmills, Basingstoke, Hampshire and New York: Palgrave Macmillan.
O'Sullivan, S. and S. Zepke (eds) (2008) *Deleuze, Guattari and the Production of the New*, London and New York: Continuum.
Panagia, D. (2006) *The Poetics of Political Thinking*, Durham, NC: Duke University Press.
—(2009) *The Political Life of Sensation*, Durham, NC: Duke University Press.
Parr, A. (2008) *Deleuze and Memorial Culture: Desire, Singular Memory and the Politics of Trauma*, Edinburgh: Edinburgh University Press.
—(2013) *The Wrath of Capital: Neoliberalism and Climate Change Politics*, New York: Columbia University Press.
—(ed.) (2010) *The Deleuze Dictionary*, Edinburgh: Edinburgh University Press.
Patton, P. (1997) "The Political Philosophy of Deleuze and Guattari", in *Political Theory: Tradition and Diversity*, A. Vincent (ed.) New York: Cambridge University Press, pp. 237–53.
—(2000) *Deleuze and the political*, London and New York: Routledge.
—(2010) *Deleuzian Concepts: Philosophy, Colonization, Politics*, Stanford, CA: Stanford University Press.
Pisters, P. (2003) *The Matrix of Visual Culture: Working with Deleuze in Film Theory*, Stanford, CA: Stanford University Press.
—(2012) *The Neuro-image: a Deleuzian Film-philosophy of Digital Screen Culture*, Stanford, CA: Stanford University Press.
Prigogine, I. and I. Stengers (1984) *Order out of Chaos: Man's New Dialogue with Nature*, New York: Bantam Books.
Protevi, J. (2000) "A Problem of Pure Matter: Fascist Nihilism in *A Thousand Plateaus*", in K. Ansell-Pearson and D. Morgan (eds) *Nihilism Now! Monsters of Energy*, London: Macmillan Press, pp. 167–88.
—(2001) *Political Physics: Deleuze, Derrida, and the Body Politic*, London and New York: Athlone Press.
—(2009) *Political Affect: Connecting the Social and the Somatic*, Minneapolis: University of Minnesota Press.
Rajchman, J. (2000) *The Deleuze Connections*, Cambridge, MA: MIT Press.
Reid, J. (2010) "On the nature of sovereignty: Gilles Deleuze and the theory of world politics", in *International Relations Theory and*

Philosophy: Interpretive Dialogues, C. Moore and C. Farrands (eds) London and New York: Routledge, pp. 119–28.

Rotman, B. (2000) *Mathematics as Sign: Writing, Imagining, Counting*, Stanford, CA: Stanford University Press.

—(2008) *Becoming Beside Ourselves: the Alphabet, Ghosts, and Distributed Human Being*, Durham, North Carolina: Duke University Press.

Saldanha, A. and J. M. Adams (eds) (2012) *Deleuze and Race*, Edinburgh: Edinburgh University Press.

Seigworth, G. (2003) "Fashioning a Stave, or, Singing Life", in *Animations of Deleuze and Guattari*, J. D. Slack (ed.) New York: P. Lang, pp. 75–106.

Serres, M. (2000) *The Birth of Physics*, Manchester: Clinamen Press.

Shaviro, S. (2009) *Without Criteria: Kant, Whitehead, Deleuze, and Aesthetics*, Cambridge, MA: MIT Press.

Slack, J. D. (ed.) (2003) *Animations of Deleuze and Guattari*, New York: P. Lang.

Smith, D. W. (2012) *Essays on Deleuze*, Edinburgh: Edinburgh University Press.

Sokal, A. and J. Bricmont (1998) *Fashionable Nonsense: Postmodern Intellectuals' Abuse of Science*, New York: Picador USA.

Stengers, I. (2000) *The Invention of Modern Science*, Minneapolis: University of Minnesota Press.

Stoner, J. (2012) *Toward a Minor Architecture*, Cambridge, MA: MIT Press.

Surin, K. (2009) *Freedom not Yet: Liberation and the Next World Order*, Durham, North Carolina: Duke University Press.

Tarde, G. (1962) *The Laws of Imitation*, Gloucester, MA, P. Smith.

—(1969) *Gabriel Tarde on Communication and Social Influence; Selected Papers*, T. N. Clark (ed.) Chicago, University of Chicago Press.

Thoburn, N. (2003) *Deleuze, Marx and Politics*, London and New York: Routledge.

Thoburn, N. & I. Buchanan (eds) (2008) *Deleuze and Politics*, Edinburgh: Edinburgh University Press.

Toscano, A. (2006) *The Theatre of Production: Philosophy and Individuation between Kant and Deleuze*, Basingstoke and New York: Palgrave Macmillan.

Tynan, A. (2012) *Deleuze's Literary Clinic: Criticism and the Politics of Symptoms*, Edinburgh: Edinburgh University Press.

Various (1987) "The Nature and Context of Minority Discourse I", *Cultural Critique*, 6, pp. 1–270.

—(1987) "The Nature and Context of Minority Discourse II", *Cultural Critique*, 7, pp. 1–224.

Voloshinov, V. N. (1986) *Marxism and the Philosophy of Language*, Cambridge, MA: Harvard University Press.
Watson, J. (2009) *Guattari's Diagrammatic Thought: Writing between Lacan and Deleuze*, London and New York: Continuum.
Widder, N. (2008) *Reflections on Time and Politics*, University Park: Pennsylvania State University Press.
—(2012) *Political Theory after Deleuze*, New York and London: Continuum.
Willat, E. and M. Lee (eds) (2009) *Thinking between Deleuze and Kant: a Strange Encounter*, London and New York: Continuum.
Williams, J. (2003) *Gilles Deleuze's "Difference and Repetition": a Critical Introduction and Guide*, Edinburgh: Edinburgh University Press.
—(2005) *The Transversal Thought of Gilles Deleuze: Encounters and Influences*, Manchester: Clinamen Press.
—(2008) *Gilles Deleuze's "Logic of Sense": a Critical Introduction and Guide*, Edinburgh: Edinburgh University Press.
—(2011) *Gilles Deleuze's Philosophy of Time: a Critical Introduction and Guide*, Edinburgh: Edinburgh University Press.
Wise, J. M. (2003) "Home: Territory and Identity" in *Animations of Deleuze and Guattari*, J. D. Slack (ed.), New York: P. Lang, pp. 107–28.
Zepke, S. (2005) *Art as Abstract Machine: Ontology and Aesthetics in Deleuze and Guattari*, New York: Routledge.
Zepke, S. and S. O'Sullivan (eds) (2010) *Deleuze and Contemporary Art*, Edinburgh: Edinburgh University Press.
Zourabichvili, F. (2012) *Deleuze: A Philosophy of the Event; Together with The Vocabulary of Deleuze*, Edinburgh: Edinburgh University Press.

INDEX

abstract machines 22, 42, 51, 62, 117
  disciplinary power 59
  faciality 85–8
  mutation 120, 122
  over-coding 120
  stratification 56–7
actual 18–22, 77, 104, 121, 152, 153
  capitalism 131
  mapping 30, 33, 137
  problems/solutions 27–8, 34, 54
  stratification 56, 62
  see also virtual
aesthetics 43, 54–5, 66, 70, 114, 138, 144–5, 151, 155 see also onto-aesthetics
affects 107–8, 111–12, 114, 145, 148
Althusser, Louis 21, 141
and, logic of 11, 36–7, 54
anthro-ethology 66, 76–92, 155
anthropology 16, 31, 66, 147
  political 115–19, 148, 157
Anti-Oedipus (Deleuze & Guattari) 1, 3–5, 10, 28–9, 33, 48, 58, 94, 99, 139, 141–2, 150, 152
  terminology 7, 20, 36, 62, 86, 132
arborescence 38, 41, 53, 86, 94, 104, 117

art 26, 34, 39, 43, 55, 70–2, 74, 85, 146–8, 151, 154–5
Artaud, Antonin 46, 96, 160n. 5
articulation 37, 63, 72, 81
  double 45, 48, 56–61, 63–4, 82
  of labor 27, 91–3
assemblage 29, 34, 37, 55, 56, 61–2, 73–4, 85, 87, 94, 99, 107, 120, 130
  economic 88–9
  territorial 68–72, 74
  see also collective assemblage of enunciation; concrete machinic assemblage
authoritarianism 29, 84
axiomatization 28, 30, 65, 129, 131–7
  revolution 119, 127, 135

Bateson, Gregory 36
becoming 35, 37, 42, 49, 56, 62, 66, 75, 88, 103–5, 138, 141, 145
  -animal 105–7
  Being 2, 8, 18–22, 30–1, 33, 35, 53, 56–7, 110–12, 136
  double- 35, 39–40, 48, 53, 105–9
  -everything of everybody 102, 113–14, 127, 136–7
  -imperceptible 110–14, 137, 144

INDEX

-minoritarian 80–1, 108–10, 114, 136–7, 157
-woman 104–9, 143, 156
being 2, 8, 11, 18–19, 21, 33, 35, 47, 54, 56–7, 111–13, *see also* becoming
Bergson, Henri 2, 5, 18, 94, 102, 146, 151, 153, 156, 159n. 2
binarization 86–7, 116
birds 25–8, 41, 46, 68–70, 72–3
bi-univocalization 37, 86–7, 116
black hole 85–7, 91–2, 99, 116, 118, 121, 133–5
body without organs 11, 31, 85, 93–101, 104, 110, 156
Boulez, Pierre 42

Canetti, Elias 95, 156
capitalism 4, 6–8, 27–8, 43–4, 65, 87, 91–3, 96, 117, 119, 122–3, 127–37, 145, 152, 153, 157 *see also* smooth capital
Capitalism and Schizophrenia (Deleuze & Guattari) 1, 93, 150
capture 7, 29, 88–91, 108–9, 117, 121, 129–30, 134–5, 137
Certeau, Michel de 47, 127, 154
Challenger, Professor 55–7, 65, 96, 103
chaosmos 21–4, 49, 54, 56–8, 75, 110–12, 148, 153
Chomsky, Noam 79
Christianity 5, 87, 91, 93, 152
Clastres, Pierre 89, 155
classicism 74
Clausewitz, Karl von 47, 127–8
coding 7–9, 28–9, 56–7, 64–5, 67–71, 73–4, 82, 86, 89, 115, 120, 131, 133–7 *see also* over-coding

collective assemblage of enunciation 22, 78–9, 82, 94–6, 112
conception (vs. execution) 124–5 *see also* labor, division of
concepts, philosophical 20, 29–30, 34–5, 37, 52, 56, 143–4, 146, 150, 153 *see also* conceptual personae
conceptual personae 26, 30
concrete machinic assemblage 22, 62, 78, 80, 82, 96, 142, 145
conjugation 119, 127, 131–6, 138
connection 10–12, 18, 35–9, 41, 73–4, 89, 99, 100, 119–20, 127, 135–8
consistency 9–11, 88, 106, 111, 126, 133–4 *see also* plane of consistency
constants 22, 77–81, 111
content 37, 55, 57–9, 62–5, 68–70, 72–4, 76, 77, 82–3, 91, 112, 131 *see also* expression
cosmos *see* chaosmos
crowds *see* herds; packs
cultural studies 140–1, 145, 147

debt 28, 87, 90, 132, 138
de-coding *see* coding
Deleuze, Gilles 1–5, 150–2
Derrida, Jacques 2, 141–2, 146, 160n. 5
desire 6–8, 20, 97–8, 100, 104, 109, 113, 119, 134
despot/despotism 28, 30, 38, 39, 43, 45, 58
  capture 89–91, 134
  segmentarity 116–17
  signifying semiotic 83–4, 93
  state-form 122–3, 130–4

de-territorialization 7, 9, 39, 53, 63–5, 69, 75, 80, 85–6, 88, 92, 99, 102, 105, 110, 120, 152
  capital 65, 131, 133–5, 137
  imperial-despotic state 83, 89–91
  music 9, 15, 73–4
  philosophy 29–30, 33–4, 40
Dialogues (Deleuze and Parnet) 11, 150
discourse, free indirect 55, 78, 148
disjunction, exclusive 70, 86
difference 2, 8–10, 23–4, 31, 42, 53, 67, 75, 80, 86, 97, 107, 110–11, 143, 146, 156
Difference and Repetition (Deleuze) 4, 8, 12, 17, 27–8, 141
double-articulation *see* articulation
Doyle, Arthur Conan 55
dualism 36, 116
Durkheim, Emile 45, 72, 119

earth 21, 30, 74, 103
ecumenon 56, 60, 63 *see also* planomenon
Engels, Friedrich 7, 135
enunciation *see* collective assemblage of enunciation
epistemology 33–53, 153–4
ethics 9, 54, 81, 93–114, 115, 142, 144, 145, 155–6
ethology 66, 69–70, 73, 75, 76, 94, 107 *see also* anthro-ethology
Euclidian geometry/space 44, 49, 160n. 3
events, philosophical 13, 34, 37, 45, 47, 87, 153

evolution 17, 19, 21–5, 30, 39–40, 51–2, 132
exchange 28, 58, 90, 116–17, 121, 130
experimentation 9, 21, 34, 40, 97, 99, 104, 134, 138
  ethics 106–7, 114
  problems 24–7, 29–30, 33
  science 51–2
expression 5, 8, 19, 80, 92, 112, 137, 154
  content 37, 55, 57–9, 62–5, 68–77, 91, 131, 134–5
  faciality 85
  problems 21, 27, 54–5
  regimes of signs 82–3
exteriority 35, 45

fabric 15, 36, 38–9, 43, 115, 117, 120
faciality 85–8, 91, 93
fascism 29, 73, 100, 102, 111, 118, 121, 157
  historical (Nazism) 121, 128
feminism 142–3, 145, 156
Fitzgerald, F. Scott 100
flows 8, 23, 51, 61–2, 65, 99, 118–21, 131–7
Foucault, Michel 2, 22, 47, 77–8, 83, 130, 141–2, 146, 154, 160n. 5
  prison-delinquency complex 58–9, 64, 72, 78, 96
frequency 42, 47, 79, 85
Freud, Sigmund 3, 5–6, 40, 93–4, 98, 150, 159n. 3

geology of morals 55–65
Guattari, Félix 1–5, 150–2

haecceities 110–14, 144
Hegel, G. F. W. 45, 145

Heidegger, Martin 2, 11, 146, 159n. 1
herds 25–6, 29–31, 90-1, 95, 105, 115
heterogeneity 37–9, 43, 49, 86, 95
historicity 18–19, 33–4, 59, 84, 130, 136–7, 145, 153
Hjelmslev, Louis 5, 37, 56–7, 77–8, 82, 153, 155, 159n. 3
homogeneity 23, 38, 43–4, 67, 77, 95, 117, 120
humans 8, 24–31, 41, 50, 65–6, 70–3, 75–6, 85, 92–4, 105–6 see also Intra-Species Social Organization Problem, human
Hume, David 5, 152, 159n. 3
Husserl, Edmund 2, 159n. 1
hylomorphism 51–2, 125, 154

ideas 34, 41, 50, 103
identity 2, 8–9, 31, 53, 86, 97, 122
image of thought 10–12, 15, 30, 35–7, 46–7, 53, 150, 152, 153
immanence 6, 21–2, 33, 35, 57–8, 84, 98, 110–14, 126, 137
improvisation 9, 16, 46, 75, 95, 100, 104, 106, 113, 124–5, 138, 152, 156 see also jazz; music
incorporeal transformations 79, 100
intensity 8, 34, 36, 40, 87, 95, 97–9, 102, 110
interiority 45, 47, 61, 68–71, 84–5
interpretation 38, 46, 83–5, 97, 99, 104, 138
Intra-Species Social Organization (ISSO) Problem 25–6, 33, 68, 71–2, 94, 105
  human 26–7, 29–30, 50, 75, 76, 88, 92, 94–5, 105, 121–3, 126, 137

James, Henry 100
jazz 9, 16, 46, 75, 106, 124–5, 152, 154, 156 see also consistency; immanence; improvisation; music; self-organization
Jung, Carl 5, 159n. 3

Kafka, Franz 11–12, 80, 101, 109, 148, 149, 150, 152
Kafka: Toward a Minor Literature (Deleuze & Guattari) 1, 5, 10, 141, 144, 149
Kant, Immanuel 3, 5–6, 10, 16–17, 21, 45, 55, 146, 148, 151, 152, 155, 159n. 4
Klee, Paul 66, 74

labor 5–7, 89–91, 117, 130–4
  division of 27, 50–2, 72, 92–3, 124–6
Labov, William 79–80
Lacan, Jacques 1–3, 5, 40, 57–8, 85, 141, 146
language 5, 18, 21–2, 27, 29, 31, 39–40, 64–6, 82, 86, 91, 117, 131, 146, 155
  linguistics 76–81
  see also Regimes of signs
law 19, 21, 48–9, 51, 125–6, 141
Lévi-Strauss, Claude 49, 116, 154
Life 13, 21–4, 26, 31
  "a" life 11
lines 39–41, 53, 100–4, 115, 119–21, 134–5

of flight 9, 84–5, 99, 106, 109–11, 117–18
linguistics *see* language
Logic of Sense (Deleuze) 3
logos 42–3, 124, 126 *see also nomos*
love 95, 97–9, 109, 111, 138

machines 10–11, 54, 87–8, 118, 120–1, 130, 133, 142, 146, 150
  mega- 90–1, 134, 137, 145, 155
  technical 54, 64–5, 96, 134
  see also abstract machines; concrete machinic assemblages; war-machines
man 21, 65, 86–7, 101, 105–9, 116
mapping 20–1, 30, 37, 40–1, 47, 81, 92, 119, 126, 137, 138, 148
Marx, Karl 3–7, 28, 131–2, 135, 141, 145, 150
Marxism 3–4, 7, 27, 57–8, 118, 130, 145, 157
masochism 97–8
mathematics 16, 19–20, 44, 58, 143, 148, 161n. 1
matter 21–3, 28, 48, 51–2, 54, 57, 61–2, 65, 74, 134
Mauss, Marcel 89, 155
May 1968 4, 118
memory 10, 18, 41, 102–4, 108, 136
metaphysics 16, 22, 53, 143, 148, 159n. 1
micropolitics 115–18, 136, 150
milieu 29–30, 34–6, 46, 48, 54, 56, 60–3, 66–74, 97, 104, 109
minor/minority/minoritarian 30, 44, 80–1, 105–8, 110, 113–14, 127, 136–8, 144, 147, 155, 156

minor science 35, 45, 48, 81 *see also* nomad science
modernism 74
molecular 61–3, 94, 101, 104–12, 115, 118–20, 154
Molecular Revolution (Guattari) 150
money 7, 27, 29, 66, 82, 88–93, 121, 129–32, 134–5, 155
motifs 67–70, 73–4, 132
multiplicities 11–12, 37–41, 94–7, 105–9, 117, 145, 156, 161n. 1
Mumford, Lewis 155
music 8–9, 15–16, 42, 46, 66–7, 73–4, 124–5, 127, 143, 151, 155 *see also* refrains

nature 19, 49, 67, 125, 154
Nazism *see* fascism, historical
Nietzsche, Friedrich 2, 5–7, 18, 25, 28, 35, 46, 114, 146, 150, 151, 153, 159n. 2, 160n. 5
Nietzsche and Philosophy (Deleuze) 2
nomadology 42, 44–53, 121–9, 145, 152, 157
nomadism 26–7, 30, 35–6, 42–8, 75, 82, 94–5, 113, 122–6, 127, 144, 145, 152, 153, 156, 157
nomad science 30, 44, 48–53, 136, 147, 152, 154
nomos 42, 124, 126 *see also logos*
non-linearity 16–22, 33, 49, 58, 87, 153, 154
noology 33, 45 *see also* image of thought

ontology 17–18, 22, 31, 54–5, 70, 151, 161n. 1 *see also* onto-aesthetics

onto-aesthetics 54–5, 63, 66, 94, 154–5
order-words 77–9, 81, 84
organism 85, 94, 98–9, 108–9, 111, 143
organization 9, 25, 27, 29–30, 51, 60–1, 63, 94, 96, 99, 110–13, 116, 118, 122, 124–6, 131 *see also* Intra-Species Social Organization Problem; plane of organization; self-organization; stratification
Oury, Jean 3
over-coding 28, 39, 44, 86, 88, 118–22, 129, 131, 133–5

packs 25–6, 30, 31, 48, 90, 94–5, 105–6, 138
painting 66, 74, 151
philosophy 12–13, 19–21, 26, 30, 34–5, 40, 47, 53, 113, 134, 136–8, 143–4, 146, 148, 152, 153
physics 16, 38, 43, 49
plane of consistency 20–1, 24, 27, 51, 53, 56–7, 60–3, 65, 85, 88, 98, 100, 104, 106, 110–14, 134, 137, 138
plane of organization 53, 56, 63, 110–12
planomenon 56, 63 *see also* ecumenon
plateaus 11, 16, 23, 33–6, 41, 87, 160n. 1
Plato 34, 43, 45, 146, 153, 160n. 6
political economy 4, 7, 43, 129, 142
politics 2–4, 9, 13, 27, 31, 39, 51–2, 54–5, 80, 87–8, 102, 109–10, 111, 115–38, 143, 144, 145, 153, 156, 157
poststructuralism 1–3, 92, 148
pouvoir see power
power 5, 11–12, 38–9, 45, 52, 58, 59, 65, 80–4, 86–9, 102, 110, 116–17, 120–2, 129, 134–7, 142, 156
  pouvoir 80–1, 107, 125, 161n. 8
  puissance 80–1, 125, 161n. 8
pragmatics 17, 20–1, 52–4, 56, 79–81, 144
primitive society 82, 86, 115–19, 130
problems 12–13, 21–2, 24–5, 27–8, 30–1, 35, 41, 45–50, 52, 54–5, 90, 136, 141, 147–8
  see also Intra-Species Social Organization (ISSO) Problem
Proust, Marcel 10–12, 39, 148, 150, 152
Proust and Signs (Deleuze) 10, 150
psychoanalysis 3, 5–7, 40, 58, 85, 93, 96–7, 104, 142, 152, 159
puissance see power

quanta 118–21, 133–5

race 48, 86, 156
reason 6, 45, 47–8, 53
refrains 15, 45, 52, 66–76, 85, 93, 101, 138, 155, 156
regimes of signs 29, 58, 65, 82–8, 92–3, 134, 142
religion 72–3, 145
rent 89–92, 132
representation 27–8, 36–8, 40, 75, 119

INDEX

resonance 79, 85, 115–18, 120, 122
re-territorialization *see* de-territorialization
rhizome 10–12, 15, 35–42, 66, 94, 103, 110, 138, 150
Rhizome (Deleuze & Guattari) 5, 10, 12
rhythm 42, 66–70, 73
Reimann, Bernhard 44, 49, 94, 148, 160n. 3
revolution 5, 7, 30, 93, 119, 127, 135–7
Rimbaud, Arthur 48
romanticism 74
royal science 30, 35, 44, 48–50, 122, 124

Sarraute, Nathalie 101
Sartre, Jean-Paul 4, 34, 85
Saussure, Ferdinand de 37, 57–8, 77, 159n. 3
schizoanalysis 5–7, 97–8, 102, 104, 141, 150, 153, 156, 157
science 12–13, 16, 39, 43, 49, 51, 58, 64, 80, 124–5, 127, 132, 144, 146, 152, 154
   and philosophy 12, 19–20, 22, 34, 53, 55–6, 136, 142, 143, 148, 152, 159n. 1
   see also nomad science; royal science
science fiction 12, 55, 148
sedentary societies 26–7, 42, 94–5
self-organization 21–5, 28–31, 39, 49, 57–8, 62, 90, 93–4, 115, 153
segmentarity 101, 104, 109, 115–22, 134–5, 157
self 10–1, 17, 84, 97–9, 114, 156, 161n. 7

semiotics 65, 76, 82–8, 91–2, 112, 122
Serres, Michel 154
sexuality 68–9, 98, 108–9, 143, 156
signs *see* regimes of signs
signification 37, 58, 79, 84–7, 99, 111–13
Simondon, Gilbert 51, 125, 154
smooth capital 43–4, 47, 93
smooth space *see* space
space 41–9, 53, 67, 91, 113, 117, 120, 122, 123–7, 133, 144, 148, 160n. 2
   vectorial 47–9
speech 18, 21–2, 77–9, 82
speed 24, 27–8, 41, 82, 92, 111–13, 154
   capital 133–4, 137
   of thought 23, 25, 30, 34–6, 40, 47, 54, 113, 134
Spinoza, Baruch 2, 5, 37, 107, 109, 114, 140, 146, 151, 159n. 2, 161n. 8
State 13, 27, 29, 42–6, 50–2, 83, 94, 105–6, 115–17, 120–2, 127–30, 136–7, 157
   capitalism 58, 91, 122–3, 128–9, 131–4
   capture 89, 129–30
   science 48–53
   see also thought, state-form of
statements 59, 77–80, 83, 96, 117
strata 22–31, 55–68, 75–6, 84–6, 88, 94, 96, 99–100, 111–12, 114, 122, 134
   mega- 22–3, 27–8, 61–5, 67, 76, 82, 92, 94, 111
stratification/de-stratification 7, 19, 29–31, 45, 53, 56–64, 75, 81, 85, 93, 96–101, 103, 110, 115, 154
striated space *see* space

structuralism 18, 21–2, 31, 37, 39, 40, 66, 77–8, 92, 146–8
subjectification 39, 78–9, 84–7, 92–3, 99, 111–13, 133–4
subjectivity 10, 17, 84–6, 90, 105, 109, 113, 143
substance 57–9, 63, 74, 77, 82–3, 85, 125
surplus 90–1, 131–2
  -labor 89–91, 132
  -value 43, 91, 117, 131–2, 135
symbolic order 27–9, 31, 66, 75–6, 88, 92

Tarde, Gabriel 119, 157
taxation 90–1, 129
territory 25–6, 61–2, 66–76, 80, 83, 85, 89, 115–17, 127–8, 130, 155 *see also* de-territorialization
thought 3, 6, 12, 23, 25–6, 29–30, 33–8, 40, 43–6, 54, 113, 134, 154
  nomad 35, 45–8, 53, 113
  state-form of 35, 43–6, 51–3, 89
  see also image of thought

time 10, 16–21, 23–4, 42, 48–9, 58, 67, 104, 111–13, 152–3

Uexküll, Jacob von 67, 107
unconscious 5–7, 40, 78, 93–6, 104, 146, 152
usage 77, 81–2

variation 8–9, 28, 47, 51, 55, 71, 77, 80–1, 126–7
virtual 12, 18–22, 27, 30, 33–4, 54, 56, 70, 77, 103–4, 106, 111, 121, 137, 152, 153
  and capital 131–2, 134
  see also actual

war 43, 123, 127–9, 137–8
war-machine 27, 29, 42–3, 45–6, 50, 81, 82, 88, 93, 109, 120, 122–3, 126–9, 137–8, 145, 157
What is Philosophy? (Deleuze & Guattari) 1, 5, 12, 19, 26, 30, 47, 137, 145, 150, 153
white wall 85–7, 91–2, 117, 133–4
wolves 25–6, 30, 70, 93–5, 105, 108, 132